Enneagram

*Tests and Results for Self Discovery
and a Journey of Transformation*

Madeleine Bougerié

[1]

presentation of the information is without contract or any type of guarantee assurance.

The trademarks that are used are without any consent, and the publication of the trademark is without permission or backing by the trademark owner. All trademarks and brands within this book are for clarifying purposes only and are owned by the owners themselves, not affiliated with this document.

TABLE OF CONTENTS

1 - ENNEAGRAM TEST - DISCOVER YOUR ENNEATYPE

The enneagram test is widely used in different fields, like the human resources selection of personnel. Awareness of your enneatype can help you understand strengths and flaws so that you can start working on emphasizing the former and improving the latter.

It's a quick test that allows you to discover your enneatype. Every question is linked to 9 possible answers, which in turn are linked to one of the enneatypes (in brackets). You must truthfully choose the answers most in line with your personality and write the corresponding number on a piece of paper.

Finally, you can look at the Enneatype that ended up corresponding to the majority of your answers in order to find out which enneatype corresponds to you.

Test

<u>1.I feel fulfilled when I am able to be:</u>

- Candid, accurate and precise (5)

- Winning, competent and concrete (3)

- Placid, balanced adequate (9)

- Optimistic, joyful and lovable (7)

- Wise, judicious and capable (1)

- Original, wise and beautiful manners (4)

- Generous, open and helpful (2)

- Stable, impartial and superior (8)

- Scrupulous and trusted (6)

<u>2. To feel good with my conscience I have</u> to:

- Have fun and enjoy life as much as possible (7)

- Helping others (2)

- Be efficient, practical and successful in my goals (3)

- Be "diligent" and do my duty (6)

- Be strong and defend the right causes (8)

- Do everything to the best of my ability (1)

- Be "different", stand out from the crowd (4)

- Know and learn as much as possible (5)

- Rest and let life flow calmly (9)

<u>3. When I am with friends:</u>

- I feel safe and imbalance even beyond my normal (9)

- I like it, but if there are many, I don't know who to choose (6)

- I immediately find something of what I did to show them (3)

- I listen to them very carefully, but without putting too much of mine (5)

- I am expansive and let myself be pampered (2)

- I always look for new stimuli to share with many different friends (7)

- I'm with who lets me talk (8)

- I find myself only with those who have a

feeling with me (4)

- I like clear and precise relationships (1)

<u>4. The image I have of me is:</u>

- I am neat and always do my homework (6)

- I am strong and authoritatively manage my relationships (8)

- I am an efficient person, who tries to do everything well (3)

- Most of the time I think I'm right (1)

- I am insightful and I understand things well (5)

- I am calm. quiet and satisfied with how my life goes (9)

- I am nice and I try to have fun and enjoy life (7)

- I move first if there is someone to help (2)

- I distinguish myself from others in everything I do (4)

<u>5. When they entrust me with an important task, I think:</u>

- I have no peace until I have realized what I have to do (1)

- They could not have chosen a better one than me and I advertise the thing (7)

- I can do it well, if it depends only on me (2)

- Why did they look for me? However I do (5)

- Depends on how I feel (4)

- I do it if I like it, otherwise I try to download it to someone (8)

- I am flattered that they have looked for me and I will do more than requested (3)

- As soon as I feel I do it (9)

- I'm afraid that they chose me because there were no others, I will get help (6)

<u>6. I willingly commit my strength to:</u>

- Fight for justice (8)

- Reach my goals (3)

- Knowing myself (4)

- Enjoy the joys of life (7)

- Live peacefully (9)

- Seeking perfection (1)

- Know what surrounds me (5)

- Collaborate with those around me (6)

- Help those around me (2)

7. <u>The thing I avoid most is:</u>

- Give in to wrath (1)

- Need someone's help (2)

- Show me what a mistake (3)

- A life without emotions (4)

- Having wrong behavior (5)

- Show my weaknesses (8)

- Clash with someone (9)

- The effort of living (6)

- The feeling of inner emptiness (7)

<u>8. During a dispute:</u>

- I try to take time to meditate on a reaction (6)

- I prevent the other from disturbing my inner balance (9)

- I fight, but only to defend myself from the strength of those in front of me (4)

- I try to avoid confrontation, most of the time it is not worth fighting (7)

- I prevent the other from taking advantage of me (5)

- I hardly admit I'm wrong (3)

- I don't make the other understand my anger (1)

- I let the other one vent (2)

- I strongly defend my reasons (8)

9. What do I think of myself when others don't understand me?

- I understand things better than others and nobody knows how many I know (5)

- I struggle every day to have my space; I have to take it, otherwise the others take advantage of it (8)

- I stand out from the rest and feel that I can't really adapt to the world around me (4)

- I am often right and things would be

better if what I say was followed (1)

- I let my world go as it goes, even if others would like me to work to change it (9)

- I love others, even if I don't receive as much as I give (2)

- I rise above the others and this makes them jealous (3)

- I am a reliable person and I am in the rules even if the others are not there (6)

- I'm happy, but I'm looking for new things because I want to be more happy (7)

Results

1. Perfectionist: cold-blooded rationalist. A honest citizen that is obsessed with the right thing. Sincere, he or she wants to be close-to-perfect and is highly critical of himself just as much as he or she is of others. Can also be very picky and pedantic.

2. Altruist: Generous and humble, he or she puts other people's needs before his or her own. Type 2 seek love and acceptance, but can also be whiny and act as victims.

3. Winner: Successful, charismatic and charming. He or she gets very mad if someone fails to recognize their greatness.

4. Artist: A writer, a painter, an actor, someone who lives by art and makes it his or her weapon. They are melancholic and might seek refuge in the past or by daydreaming of the. They have a thing for strange situations, as well as scandals and anything that is forbidden.

5. Investigator: Focused, meticulous, innovative, an introvert and a great listener;

someone who is calm and might come across as cold or distant because he or she doesn't allow himself or herself to become emotionally involved.

6. Defender: A very responsible and committed individual who is also reliable and compassionate. They do not like people who are uncertain and unreliable. They can be very suspicious.

7. Enthusiast: A very optimistic person who is usually energetic and outgoing, very popular and always willing to try new experiences, looking for fun. It's in their nature to try to escape unpleasant situations and feelings.

8. Leader: Someone who loves challenges. Type 8 feels and act as a leader even when he or she isn't. They are usually very strong and confident, displaying a dominant personality. They can also be provocative and quarrelsome, resulting in them making people afraid.

9. Mediator: Someone who is calm and patient, very unpretentious. They usually avoid conflict and see the best in people, but can also be influenced fairly easily.

2 – ENNEATYPES

2.1 Enneagram Type 1

He is defined as the perfectionist. The perfectionist is that type of personality who tries to improve things since he considers that nothing is sufficiently perfect, and therefore, there is room for improvement in everything.

They are idealists who strive to put chaos in order and are very attentive to detail. They are always attentive to their mistakes and those of others. They need to improve everything, and this can be good in some cases but counterproductive in others.

The inability to achieve perfection, in eneatype 1, makes him feel guilty for not being up to some situations and also feeds his anger against imperfections in general.

Generally, anger is expressed in the form of impatience, frustration, a sense of annoyance, criticism, and judgment.

Although generally, this Enneatype is kind-hearted, the anger that builds up can lead to occasional attacks. Those who have the most marked characteristics can also be intractable, while the "healthier" ones can be loyal, responsible, and very capable friends. They are people of strong and healthy principles who follow the rules. Unfortunately, they expect others to do the same.

They are generally practical, well-organized, hard-working, honest, and respectful people. They are more practice-oriented, organized, honest, and respectful, but their continuous commitment to improve and the attention paid to detail continually makes it difficult to relax. They always place duty before pleasure.

Emotionally they tend to be repressed, and it is very difficult for them to express feelings of sweetness. Typically they see emotion as a sign of weakness and lack of control. On some occasions, due to perfectionism, enneatype 1 can be confused with enneatype 5, which, unlike type 1, which tends to anger, tends instead to worry and anxiety.

Key trends:

They want to be right (according to their parameters). They continually strive to improve everything, to be consistent with their ideals, and to be able to justify themselves and their conduct. They try to put themselves in the position of not being criticized by anyone.

When it is healthier:

Reliable and responsible, he likes to keep

the traditions and things that are done in the right way. Respect the agreements. It radiates security and is available to help others.

Lost quality:

The ability to be in a good mood, laugh and have fun activities

Fixation:

Perfectionism. Nothing is perfect enough; it can be improved.

The perfectionism of Enneatype 1 could be defined as an interest in the moral principles, ideals, and needs of a very strong superego. Also, in the interpersonal plane, it is a tool of manipulation and domination. This is because these rules are defended with so much impetus and are imposed on others and serve to hide personal desires and needs.

Breaking point:

Embittered character people disappoint him over and over again.

What they should avoid:

Avoid the tendency towards enterotype 4; in that case, the enterotype 1 would be taken by constant moodiness and irrationality.

Basic component: Wrath

Wrath is inherent in the depth of the structure of this personality. It could be described as a resentment caused by a feeling or feeling of injustice. The latter is generated when these people strive to do things "well" while believing that the rest of the world is not trying hard enough. Anger presents itself as irritation, reproach, and hatred, although, for the most part, it remains unexpressed because these people tend always to maintain a virtuous image of themselves.

Self-image: I change things...

The vision of himself as a person who improves the environment around him with his own effort and his ethical and moral values. Consider yourself as an Effective worker and person trustworthy.

Fears: Fear of not being right, of being unsuitable.

The perfectionist wants and strives to do "correct" things. He is afraid that his ideas are wrong and counterproductive. He is afraid of being bad, corrupt, perverse, or imperfect.

Deep Desire: Feeling Perfect.

Doing things "well" and being a "correct" person is what eneatipo 1 needs to feel "worthy."

Distortion of desire:

The desire for integrity degenerates into excessive and unhealthy perfectionism.

How he manipulates others:

By correcting others and insisting on convincing them of their criteria and values.

His justification:

He justifies himself by appealing to "correctness" or to the things he believes are correct.

How it attacks others:

By being afraid of being bad, unsuitable, corrupt, or defective in some aspect, they try to show evil, corruption, and defects in others.

Defense mechanism:

For the moral ethics of Enneatype, 1 certain thought and desires are unacceptable. For this reason, he tries to cover them and deny them to himself by means of a continuous action against them and trying to generate the opposite image in order to suppress certain sensations.

Neurotic features in Enneatype 1:

Discipline: Worker, responsible, obsessive, and serious.

Criticism: As a way of expressing anger, he wants to rationalize, deny, and justify.

Self-criticism: The difficulty of self-acceptance, devaluation of himself, and others hid under the guise of good and virtuous.

Domain: Assertive, authoritarian, rigid, haughty, the role of superiority. He has a passion for being right.

Moralist: Judge, reformer, rigid, and puritanical. It requires himself and others to put duty first and pleasure later.

Control: He controls his emotional exposure a lot, repressed.

Demanding: With himself and with others, he tends to give sermons and teach takes on the role of savior.

The ideology of the Enneatype 1

Unhealthy Ideas: If I am perfect, I am worthy of love, I am worth it, and I can be accepted. It is absolutely necessary to control emotions and instincts. One should not act spontaneously or out of control.

I can't delegate and trust anyone. I don't take responsibility, and I do things, nobody will do them any good.

We must seek good and fight evil, duty before pleasure. Nobody gives anything for nothing; self-sufficiency is better. Effort, sacrifice, and discipline are needed to do things well.

We need to do justice, change the world. Perfection must be sought. What I think is truth, I'm right, and the others are wrong.

Healthy ideas:

Sometimes things are as they are, it is better to accept them than to try to correct or perfect them so that they adapt to our beliefs of how they should be.

Things are already perfect. The concept of "perfect and imperfect" of "good and bad" is a concept created according to my beliefs and takes me away from the truth.

I do what I can do, and others do the same. I have my reasons, but the others have theirs and can be equally valid.

Everything makes sense and has its place, even if there are things I can't understand. I can wake up from judgment and be less demanding, leave me alone, and leave others alone.

I can also be accepted by being spontaneous, without effort to look better. It is better to accept things as they are and to flow with the current of life.

How Enneatype 1 reaches serenity (virtue):

Serenity is the acceptance of oneself and others. Cultivate the faith that things can succeed well without much control and effort. Stop correcting others.

Evolution is learning to see things in its beauty. Find the good in things, events, and people.

Let go of criticism and self-criticism,

abandon claims to yourself and others. Actively cultivate goodwill.

Start by accepting anger and mistakes. Accept the world as it is. Trust in nature and try to be serene, selfless, and impartial.

Give yourself the right to be yourself and accept your mistakes and those of others. Stop doing and connect to your inner child, respect the impulses, do not worry so much, and trust that nature is good and wise, that something superior supports us. Afford more pleasure.

Socially:

Let go, accept mistakes, make mistakes, and flow with more freedom and spontaneity. Look inward in your own intimacy, connect with your body, and accept emotions and needs, share as an equal.

In the sexual sphere:

Reassuring oneself, channeling one's emotions, seeing the other's needs more and accepting it, containing the impulse to correct. Calm the impetus and anger by connecting more with pain and vulnerability. Cultivate patience.

To learn more about the Enneagram, we took inspiration from these books.

Towards improvement:

Become aware that works without pauses. When a sportsman trains too much, he can go to a stage where he experiences symptoms of "overtraining." These symptoms decrease his sporting performance. The only solution to this is to rest. In the same way, L'eneatipo 1 should do, rest, calm the alarm bell ready to criticize, do not try to continually work hard to improve everything, try to flow, and also dedicate yourself to healthy recreation. Enneatype 1 must become aware that perfection is impossible and that it is not that inner voice that always drives him to perfect everything. He is not that voice (the superego) that continually pushes him to criticize others or that continues to tell him to keep the composed and rigid attitude during the day to appear something that is not really. Being is different from appearing; it should give space to its true being so it can achieve happiness.

If you are an enneatype 1, let go, relax, and trust others too. You cannot transform into your ideal; it is impossible to get to be everything we imagine. You have to accept things and people as they are. Identify your emotional needs; you definitely have them like every human being. You have the right to be worried or sad. You can show your needs and ask other people for help. Having vulnerabilities does not mean being weak; it means being human.

Recognize and express your anger. Do not

swallow it, or hold it, throw it out of your body, transform it into something positive, such as sport, meditation, stretching, art. Express yourself. Do not repress yourself.

Sometime during childhood, one has gained the conviction that only perfection is lovable. You have to earn the right to be loved. It is difficult for ONE to imagine that the imperfect and broken love deserve love. But it is precisely this experience that helps them to make a breakthrough: unconditional love. You can't believe that. You can see how Paul and Martin Luther deal with it because they are both one.

He or she is constantly disappointed by the reality because it always hopes: Now something perfect is finally coming! This disappointment condenses into anger. It is not the anger at something specific, but formless, universal anger, the anger about the imperfection of the world.

This anger provides them with a lot of energy to try to improve the world. But it is aggressive energy. Everyone often does the right thing with the wrong motives. Discovering that is very humiliating! God uses our sins for God's purposes. Therefore, "no flesh can boast of God," as Paul says.

Their anger does not look like anger. At first glance, it looks like idealism or zeal. It works like a virtue. And this anger is hidden not only from others but also from the one itself. One is usually surprised when they find out that their sin is anger. Others usually see it more than they do. They are convinced that they have high ideals and noble goals. It is very difficult for them to admit that these are only their noble ideals and not necessarily objectively noble goals. They have to recognize this first of all if they want to be merciful.

Deep in one is a deep stream of anger that she doesn't recognize or admit. This current leads to this. That one makes quick judgments. This happens so quickly that they do not even notice that they have already made another judgment. These quick judgments eventually condense into a permanent state of resentment. It happens in a flash: anger - judgment resentment. Anger - judgment - resentment. Therefore, they have to grab at first when the trouble arises. This is the only way to break the vicious cycle. You have to realize how deep and constant this anger is. And they have to stop naming them differently, such as "truth" or "justice." You just have to admit that they're fucking angry. It is very difficult for them because model children are not angry.

The self-image on which one depends is: "I am a good child!" Because they had to be model children to either get their parents' love or not to lose them. For example, you must not allow yourself to be selfish. That is why their selfishness has to disguise themselves. Do not allow yourself to perceive your own feelings, but feel what you should feel. That's why her feelings are hidden - even for herself.

One must first discover its true feelings and its own view of reality. This is very difficult because everything is constantly overlaid and suppressed by commands and prohibitions. The ONE must stop making judgments, especially moral judgments. ONE is obsessed with moral judgments. Everything must be good or bad, meritorious, or sinful. If you learn to let things be as they are, if you learn to see before you judge - you will achieve a wonderful serenity.

If things go well, they end up overcoming and transforming anger better than anyone else. At some point, they are so tired of their anger and strained seriousness that their inner peace can become their greatest gift. The redeemed ONE has a pronounced sense of harmony and balance.

Usually, you think of him or her as very reasonable people. Because their judgments allow them to see both sides. But they have to stop judging all the time. You have to stop believing in your anger. They have to stop thinking that their judgments are really aimed at the truth. Instead of "all or nothing," they must allow "both-and". That is redeeming for ONE.

2.2 Enneagram Type 2

They are people who have a good image of themselves. Love is their highest ideal. For them, love can do everything, and for love, everything is worth it. They are warm and emotional people who care a lot about their personal relationships, devote a huge amount of energy to this, and hope to be appreciated for their efforts.

They usually participate in society with a social conscience and are extroverted. They are the kind of people who remember everyone's birthday and go above and beyond to help a colleague, spouse, or friend. They are people who usually thrive in the helping professions. They have tact with people; they perceive them emotionally.

It is essential for them to be able to help others: it is a gesture that makes them feel good about themselves and, above all, important.

Individuals belonging to enneatype 2 are convinced of their lack of interest, and it is true that they are often genuinely available and worried about others. It is also true, however, that these people need to feel needed.

But the love they give is not entirely without reason; damage to receive. Ennatypes 2 tend to develop a sense of law when it comes to people closest to them. Since they sacrificed themselves for others, they begin to feel indebted to them.

They can be manipulative and attempt to command others: they feel fully justified in doing so because they "have earned the right," and their intentions are good. The darker side of enneatype 2 appears when they begin to feel that they will never receive the love they deserve for all their efforts. In such circumstances, they can become hysterical and irrational.

Because they tend to help others meet their needs, they can forget to take care of themselves. This can lead to physical wear and emotional exhaustion. Enneatypes 2 need to learn that they can be of real help to others only if they are healthy, balanced, and focused on themselves. These individuals feel bad about themselves if they don't play an obvious role in helping someone in their life.

Key trends

They want to be loved, and they want to be necessary for others, to make others respond before them.

When it is healthy

He knows how to give warmth and support; he likes to help and comfort those who suffer; he likes that others need him and willingly makes himself available to others. He likes to laugh and see others happy. He appreciates that there is the affection in relationships and puts love in what he does.

When it is not healthy

Lost quality: the ability to contact your needs, recognize them and ask for help (E4)

Fixing: redundancy. "I have so much to give ..." "I need ..."

Passion: pride

As he does everything with good intentions, he ignores criticism and does not recognize his shortcomings. When the cheerful enneatype 2 tends towards enneatype 8, they become aggressive and dominant.

Characteristics of type 2

I think: they only see me if they are wonderful. They have a form of superiority above good and evil They are free, spontaneous, sensual.

There is no need to compete; they already feel the best. They praise and are generous but to confirm that they are divine. They can be very capricious and explorers of the other.

Manipulators

They need to feel necessary and desired. He neglects his own needs in order not to know his true self or essence. They believe it is a privilege that others relate to them.

Freedom is very important to them. They are very chaotic minds. The defects are not seen. They take a lot of confidence. They are very critical and see where the weak points to hurt.

They believe they had a happy childhood and it didn't happen. They confuse desire satisfaction with love (if you satisfy me, you love me). Confusion of desire with the necessity to go to therapy; they go for personal development.

They usually have a seductive father and an overprotective mother. They fall in love and bark quickly when something is wrong.

They are above the rules of good and evil. They ask a lot and don't give much. They are very theatrical, very manipulative. They tend towards action rather than thinking.

Fixation

Life is gorgeous (false abundance). They overestimate love and emotions.

They have the idea that everything is loving, always justified by love. "I praise you because you praise me."

They promise more than what they give, they think they give more than what they give, and that's their problem

Neurotic patterns of Enneatype 2

Passion: pride

The "pride" of enneatype 2 can be understood as an imaginary exaltation of one's value and attractive power. These are people who have a good self-image. They tend to be considered "more gifted" than others. They deny many of their needs by trying to "help" others.

Overabundance

It is the rationalization of pride. It is the thought for which they support their sense of grandeur.

Desire

Feeling loved. Enneatype 2's need to feel special is satisfied by the love of the other. It is the other who confirms his inflated sense of his worth. The fact that this confirmation is accomplished with love corresponds to the childish frustration they have suffered.

Distortion of Desire

The desire to be loved degenerates into the need to be needed.

Self Image

I help. They see themselves as people who help others. Helping others makes them feel great. But this help is selective, only for those who consider it. Behind this "help," you can hide a neurotic "give to receive."

Fear

For his self-image of self-magnification and generosity in helping others, he fears that he too has needs (emotional and affective needs); this could indicate that its size is not such. His greatest fear is that of being unworthy of love and of driving away from his friends and loved ones.

Way to handle others

Discovering the needs and desires of others, thus creating addictions.

Justification: service.

He explains his actions as selfless gestures.

The individuals of enneatype 2, fearing that they are neither desired nor loved, make others feel unworthy of giving love, generosity, or attention.

Defense mechanism

Repression refers to the mechanism that prevents certain internal impulses or desires from becoming aware. By responding to these impulses, but without recognizing them in a cognitive way, one can have an attitude of irresponsibility and give an impression of falsehood.

Nevrotic Characteristics:

He wishes to be special and to feel better than others.

Need for love, delicate sensitivity. He needs erotic love: tenderness and possessiveness. Seduction wise, there's an effort in being warm, attractive. It seduces those it perceives as valuable people.

Assertive, dominate, subdue. Strong momentum and disinhibition.

Hedonism, pleasure-oriented character. The difficulty is facing pain, conflict, and frustration.

Histrionic, makes scenes to attract attention or get away with it. It does not accept rules or limits. Susceptible.

An opportunist who gives to receive, helps to feel important. He gets angry if his wishes are not met.

Ideas of enneatype 2

As I am special and better than others, I deserve love and appreciation. I always have a lot of love to give. Love is the most important thing in this life.

If you want me, you have to desire me, satisfy my whims, and guess what I want. Those who contradict me or judge me don't want me. I seduce and enjoy myself because I am very attractive. I don't need the other, but they need me. I need to feel necessary.

I have to be important to be happy because I deserve it. I have to be independent, better than others depend on me.

If someone loves me, I must be the most

important thing for him/her and must always be available for me.

The pain is unbearable; it can destroy me; it is better to seek pleasure.

Healthy Ideas:

It is best to accept and recognize your limits. I don't have to try so hard to look special to be loved.

Frustration and pain are part of life; things cannot always happen according to my wishes. I can accept pain and pleasure.

I don't need to try very hard to seduce and attract everyone. Love is important, but so is wisdom, creativity, and other values. I also have needs. I can ask for help or advice and recognize my shortcomings.

I can devote myself to experience and

accept what life brings me. I can count on the fact that things flow naturally without having to manipulate reality.

I can accept that some people love me and others don't.

Virtue of Enneatype 2: Humility

Humility is to recognize one's own truth and share it with others without falling into enlarging one's image, that is, recognizing mistakes and ignorance, accepting criticism.

Humility is simplicity, freeing grandeur, and understanding that you are one of many.

Let go of the dependence on love and pleasure, accept that pain exists, that things don't always go as you want. Recognize the shortcomings, what is missing, learn to ask instead of demanding.

Attitudes that Improve Enneatype 2

He must be more aware of the effort he continually makes to please others and must not give much value to how they perceive him.

It must be remembered that it is impossible to please everyone. Furthermore, it is not said that others already express a possible liking in the way we expect it; they can do it in a more subtle way or simply in a different way.

Be honest with people. Do not compliment systematically and do not engage in other manipulative behaviors to conquer people. Don't make yourself completely available to others. You can help them, but to a certain extent, that it is not an "all or nothing." Remember that the first person you need to help and take care of is you.

Don't give too much selflessly; maybe you will miss it later. Be aware of what are the real reasons that drive you to help or give to others. Learn to become aware of the process of "giving in order to receive" and / or whether there is a search for wanting to feel good as a reason for beneficial actions towards others.

Be aware that your pride compensates for an unconscious feeling of not being desired. A greater dose of pride and arrogance means that the person suffers more from that feeling of not being wanted. Your attitude must be more realistic and, therefore, more humble, but without falling into false humility, which is also a form of pride.

Be aware of your limitations; you cannot "everything." You too are human, in flesh and blood, you get tired, and you need rest. Make sure you respect your limits.

Overwhelming love

The ZWEI believed at some point that it would be loved if it loved itself: "If I can serve you, you will love me!" That is why TWOs seek security in the world of love. They go through life and buy love. They make you have to love them. They flatter themselves: "I will love you in a way that you cannot love me! And if you still do not love me, then you will feel guilty!" They don't even notice how much pressure and feelings of guilt they convey. But everyone who belongs to the environment of a TWO feels this constant silent expectation. We always know that this person expects more attention and is looking for more reaction.

Helper of the world

TWO are lovers, servants, and helpers of

the world. This love takes many different forms. TWO are also the co-dependents of this world. If you are loved by a co-addict, one day, you have to pay for it. Because there is always an intent that is hidden even from the TWO itself. A fish hook and a string are attached to this love. When the TWO realizes this, it begins to become free.

Own needs

The ZWEI has a deep sense of shame, ZWEIer discovers early on how needy they are and at no cost want anyone to find out how deep this need is and how much they need others. That is why they operate indirectly. They often fulfill their needs in secret. In this, they become masters. You really give a lot. But they keep a secret record of it. They send out countless Christmas cards and keep an internal list of who sends them one.

Chocoholic

If one day you are fed up with not being left behind as others love you, you decide: " I deserve a reward! "They reward themselves in a very real, albeit often secret way. Often they are chocolate alcoholics. They have to get sweets after giving away so many sweets. But sometimes they are ashamed of it and hide the chocolate under the bed. Often go they go to a shop and buy something they don't really need, but they are ashamed of their needs.

Self-image

It is important that TWO face the fact how deep their need and shame are so that their love becomes more popular Light comes and becomes more honest, you have to learn to laugh at your exaggerated need, When they realize that much of their love has been dishonest, it is a deeply humiliating experience. At ZWEIer, I experienced more than anyone else how they cried uncontrollably when their pattern became clear to them. Because her self-image has always been: "I am love in person!" If this picture is suddenly taken away, it almost tears it up.

Humility

Here you can see what their sin, arrogance is about and what the path to humility means to them. They have to get to the sobering point where they understand: "I myself am not capable of loving at all. I have to withdraw and allow God to love through me"When you learn that, you become very humble tools of love. But first, you have to recognize and let go of your own fishing hooks. This is a heroic conversion for a TWO. If

TWO stops are counting up, it is free.

Wonderful friends.

The gift of Cordiality is, at the same time, the trap of the TWO. It takes a long time for the heart to be purified. The simplest way to describe the way of redemption of a TWO is as follows: It is about the purification of the world of feelings and relationships. When TWO goes this way, they are very lovable. Such people are wonderful friends. Detect

Manipulation

But the rest of us, too, have to be careful not to manipulate the TWO on our part. They are not only manipulative but also very manipulative. We all know that and use it wisely. We know we only have to say to a TWO: "I need you!" - and she'll jump. TWO even know they do. So they hate themselves for it afterward. And they hate you too because they know you are taking advantage of them. The rest of us also need to be converted in relation to the TWO, because it is a co-dependency. We benefit from the TWO and want to keep them as they are. That's why we also have to say goodbye to this game. Especially in marriages, it is often the ZWEI partner who does not want that. Because it's also convenient

2.3 Enneagram Type 3

The Enneatype Three will strongly identify with this situation:

Being the best at what he does is a strong driver for him, and over the years, he has received much recognition for what he has achieved. He gets a lot done, and he is successful in almost all the things he tackles. He strongly identifies with what he does because he believes that your value is based on what you achieve and the recognition you receive for it. He always has more to do than is possible in the available time, so he often puts his feelings and self-esteem aside to get the job done. He becomes impatient when people don't use their time properly. If someone else is too slow to execute a project, he would rather just take over. He feels that he is in control of every situation, and that is how he comes across.

Further personality traits of the Three:

The Three are diplomatic, charming, and ambitious, and when a new experience arises, he first wonders whether it is useful to him. He is more focused on a goal than on relationships and sets his feelings aside to do a job. He often has the need to perform well, does not want to depend on others; he does things his way. De Drie believes it is important to let people know what he is good at and Core qualities, pitfalls, and allergies. Each type has its own core qualities. If this core quality is applied too strongly, it becomes a pitfall, and others experience this as deviant behavior. And each type is allergic to certain types of behavior of others and reacts to it from its pitfall.

Core Qualities:

Pitfall

Allergy

Challenge

Passion

Fanaticism

Laziness

Relaxation

Targeting

Possession

Halfheartedness

Dosing

Optimism

Superficiality

Doom thinking

Deepness

Decisiveness

Short-sightedness

Resignation

Reflection

Recommendations for the Three:

- Moderate your pace

- Welcome your feelings

- Understand that a mistake is not a disaster

- There is always love for you, not only when you accomplish something

- Work on sincerity and honesty and never

forget that it is your nature is to enjoy your life and to respect and appreciate others.

The ultimate challenge for the Three:

Recovers the true truth that love comes to you for what you are and not for what you do. Qualities of the Essence are the pursuit of the higher idea: the regaining of hope and the higher virtue: sincerity (honesty).

Spirituality

Based on their assumption that appreciation depends on image and status, the Threes deceive themselves by taking hope out of their own performance rather than work that comes from universal principles. According to the spiritual view, hope gives us strength and direction to support our actions. Hope can carry our heart, and it has its origin in our unconscious instead of in our conscious desires. The projection of the image of a successful person takes the place of a genuine (honest) self-image with the Three, and vanity inflates his personal merits. Deception is necessary to maintain the image of a successful person.

The result

The Three is praised at a very young age for what he does, especially by the mother. Not for what he is, like the Two, but for what he couldn't do all of them. For example, he has to do everything well at school. As a result, he will perform to get the compliment from his mother. It is a much-played role in our culture and the most appreciated. The child works on a positive identification with the mother.

The dilemma

Three of them felt loved for what they did instead of what they felt. 'Doing' was appreciated instead of 'feeling.' The image was appreciated instead of depth. To thrive in this environment, children of the Three types learned to perform well and to increase their success.

He is a very motivated go-getter, can handle details very well, finds it important to be appreciated and admired, and finds it normal if he is the center of attention.

The Three does not feel comfortable with long-term obligations, so he makes things easy for himself with important changes in life. He is confident and driven to excel and enjoys working on things that give the opportunity for reward and personal recognition. Over the years, he has changed his values and lifestyle several times. In the first meeting, he is balanced, cool, and reserved, although he does his utmost to meet people and establish relationships. When he is angry, he usually becomes aloof, and when he doesn't like people, he usually remains friendly despite his feelings. He attaches great importance to doing things better than others and is proud of his flexibility; what is suitable or important often changes.

The Three are rarely restrained by self-doubt, but when confronted with someone, he usually turns around too much. When he feels insecure, he becomes arrogant and dismissive, and serious setbacks make him numb and determined. He avoids intimacy if he fears that he cannot meet the expectations of others.

The Basis

In the period from half of the pregnancy to one year after the birth, the essential basic conclusions are determined that form the child to a certain Enneatype. During this period, the child develops his physical identity and fights between 'Trust in' and 'Suspicion of,' a basic bipolar need, or a developmental polarity. This development focuses on the urge for the survival of the individual, and the motor of this urge to survive is the development of fear, whereby experiencing fear leads to a certain action for self-preservation (the conclusion of life). If this action works, this becomes THE solution for the child, and this solution determines the development towards the structure of a certain Enneatype.

Lost Life Essence of the Three

The small child was in distress when he felt that he could no longer meet the standards, values

, and excessive admiration of the mother.

The connection with the sense of universal hope that everything that needs to be done proceeds according to universal laws and principles.

Compensatory Belief

The world rewards Doing, not Being. To be loved, you focus on "Do Good" instead of just "Being a Man."

Ensure that things are carried out, go for success, and a good image because love is only given if your achievements are approved. Focus on tasks and goals and put an urgency in the work with little attention to one's own feelings.

Desire and its distortion to be valuable. This degenerates into the pursuit of success.

Core identification of the Three

Strongly identifies himself with a self-image that has developed on the basis of what he holds for admiration by others. Resists acknowledging and acknowledging feelings of emptiness and his own self-rejection. Admirable, desirable, attractive, excellent, well-adjusted, effective, with 'limitless possibilities.

The mental drive of the three is vanity

Pitfalls for the Three

The belief that being super-efficient guarantees success, recognition, love, and acceptance.

Fearing that they are worthless themselves, the Three give others the feeling of being worthless by treating them arrogantly or with contempt.

Emotional Passion

(Self) deception to achieve the goal by posing in a different way, always having a 'Successful' story ready, presenting 'Successful,' and deceiving oneself about one's own feelings. Deceiving by believing that one is exclusively ego. With this belief, all efforts are focused on the development of the ego rather than on our true nature. This passion can also be called vanity, an attempt to make the ego think that it is valuable without turning to the spiritual source.

Significant traits

Core belief: I am what I propose

Defense: identification

Intuition tailored to approval for performance

What the Three does not want, avoidance: failure

Emotional Orientation: (self) deception

Fixations: vanity Work

Motivation: impulses from outside

Main themes of the Three:

Emphasizes that it is efficient, capable, and outstanding. Focuses on goals, a pragmatic approach, and the science of how to present.

Moves with feelings to continue to focus on tasks through repression and his attention, to remain active. Performing keeps painful feelings under control. It looks for feelings signals in others.

In relation to systems, they want to cooperate with the system. But they are just as happy to withdraw from it; they interpret the rules as they like and cheat.

They learned to compete, do different activities at the same time, and promote themselves. They learned how to impress others. Because being successful was a way to get love, they learned to build a facade of success around them. An image can be misleading. Instead of making their own needs clear, they tune in to achieving results. In response to changes in the situation, they adjust their self-presentation. They become perfect lovers, efficient 'doers,' the managers in the department.

As long as they are good in the eyes of others, they have a good feeling about themselves, even though they have difficulty making contact with their own feelings. Because they cannot be guided by the power of their own emotions, they will naturally take over the emotional guidance of others. They look at what others expect from them, and then they respond to this. If it turns out that a certain image gives them something, they adopt the characteristics that belong to a certain role.

They do not realize that they only convey an image.

They only know that they hate it when they are not loved; that others like them when they come across successfully; that they can change their self-presentation and that it seems that others like them more if they are doing well. If this habit becomes automatic, their self-observation stops.

They then become the victims of total self-deception and are no longer able to distinguish their own feelings from the feelings that the image entails. They only know that they hate it when they are not loved; that others like them when they come across successfully; that they can change their self-presentation and that it seems that others like them more if they are doing well. If this habit becomes automatic, their self-observation stops.

Successful Workers grow by seeing themselves apart from their image. When they see how they praise themselves, exaggerate their performance, and adjust their way of making an impression on others, they are free to choose how they want to respond. They are supported by people who reformulate the goals of relationships from emotional appearances to emotional depths, who understand their habit of avoiding their own feelings, who are loyal to them and are not fooled by their convincing façade.

The Child Soul of the Three

The Six is the center of the Three, so behind the efficient and controlled layer of a Three is a very anxious child. Shy, timid, insecure, and scared as it is, this child-soul experiences the world as a hostile and malevolent place. Others are threatening; sometimes in such a way that he can develop paranoia that they want to catch him and no matter how much a Three has achieved and no matter how much outward success he has achieved, he still experiences himself deep down as one of the weaklings in the struggle for the existence. In fact, all attempts by the Three to achieve something can be seen as a reaction to a frightened child-soul, an attempt to overcome this part of himself and to defend himself against it. This explains why all the success is never enough for him. No matter how great his status or power is, if he does not process and integrate his child-soul, the inner fear and uncertainty can never be resolved. From the child-soul perspective, the image of a Three is an attempt to camouflage this frightened and immature part of itself.

For the development of a Three, it is necessary that he tackles this child-soul, who experiences the ground under his feet as naturally unstable and unsupportive. As he increasingly recognizes his fear and realizes how powerful it is in his psyche, his frightened child will feel inner cherished and, therefore, more secure. Allowing itself will, over time, transform its fear into inner trust, support, and well-being, and the Three will understand exactly what these qualities were that he had as a young child, and that was not allowed and supported by his early environment. It may be that his original embodiment of essential "Will" was threatened by circumstances in the family and eventually worn down, or the ease with which he could do things made him a target of envy and hatred of his parents or the other children, thereby undermining his confidence. Apart from psychodynamics, the inner ground of a Three, as his child-soul is integrated into his consciousness, will feel more secure and stronger.

A Winner is the personality of the Enneagram who considers themselves the most successful. In addition, failure or failure is viewed by the Winner as a threat to psychological survival. This failure is kept away from consciousness through defense mechanism identification.

A Winner also referred to as Motivator, will enter a room in which, for example, a reception is being held, as follows. As the Winner enters the room, it will be unconsciously observed who receives the most appreciation or attention in that room. If this is a professor or a sports star, then the Winner will talk and behave as a very well-read and knowledgeable person or as a person who has also performed the necessary sports performances. Behavior and identity are subconsciously distorted to appear as successful as possible. Feelings of the actual and possibly lesser self-worth are hereby not allowed into the consciousness. Here too, this type of defense will ultimately no longer suffice. The outside world can regard this behavior as 'plastic.'

Your strength is, at the same time, your biggest pitfall.

If you use that too much and are not attuned to the other, the other will experience that power negatively and will respond with resistance.

The strengths of the Three:

- Works very effectively

- Is focused on success

- Has self-discipline

- Can handle attention well

- Makes himself loved by performance

- Want to be the best

- Goals and results are important

- Self-presentation is changed to get better
results

- Put his heart in the work

- Focus all attention on his task

- Think versatile

- Get a lot done by thinking task-oriented

- Is a good organizer

- Is the leader of the winning team

Threes are strongly focused and driven to perform and identify with what they do. With the move to Nine, they can end up under their ruthless pursuit of success. The drive of Threes to distinguish and prove themselves inevitably results in stress and conflicts in their relationships. At such moments they can take it slower; they become more diplomatic and more lenient, like the average Nines. Three on the Nine still want to stand out from the crowd, but not too much either. The profile themselves less and do not try to stand out too much, among others.

In their pursuit of success, three of them often end up in situations in which they are forced to do things that they actually do not find very interesting. For a limited time, this does not cause any problems, but if they have a career or relationship for a long time that is not based on what they really want, it leads them not to feel involved and let it all go by, like Nines.

Instead of working efficiently, they fill their time with irrelevant activities and routines, hoping to roll through difficult situations unharmed. While Threes usually handle tasks quickly and efficiently and respond attentively to others, they are uninterested and complacent under stress.

In the event of failures or major setbacks in their careers, Thies may believe that their last hour has struck. During such periods, they become disillusioned with life and themselves. Their underlying void breaks through, and they make an apathetic and burned out impression. Instead of taking steps to improve their situation with their undeniable decisiveness, they tend to avoid the reality of their problems and waste their time with wishful thinking and fantasizing about their next big success.

If Threes have gone through a serious crisis or have been chronically abused in their youth, they can make the fall down to the unhealthy aspects of their type.

Setbacks that inflict serious dents on his self-confidence can cause the Three to come to the frightening insight that he has built his life on a weak or even false foundation. He may be afraid that he is actually failing, or that his successes are of no value, or that his claims about himself are fraudulent. And his fear may be partly justified. The moment he sees the truth in these fears, he can take the road to health and liberation. On the other hand, he could do even harder to maintain his illusion of superiority and double deny that he suffers or has any problem. ("No problems! I'm fine; I do everything I can to get ahead").

If the Three perseveres in this position, he can make the fall down to the unhealthy levels.

If you notice that you or someone you know shows the warning signs (see warning signs) for a longer period of time (longer than a few weeks), then it is highly recommended that you go into therapy or call in other help.

Warning signs for the Three in Need

Potential pathology: narcissistic personality disorder, nervous pressure, depression (often anhedonia), narcissistic anger and revenge, psychopathic behavior. Further recognition points:

Physical exhaustion and being burned out (burnout) as a result of relentless work addiction.

Strengthening the false self-image and

increased dishonesty and deceit. Emotional poverty and inner emptiness. Attempts to conceal the level of emotional distress. Jealousy and unrealistic success expectations

Self-advertising and opportunism, serious episodes of anger and hostility.

The Three at rest and his performance point (the direction of integration):

Three people realize themselves and remain healthy by learning to dedicate themselves, like healthy Sixes, to others and to goals that go beyond their self-interest. Their focus shifts from the need to maintain a self-image to the deeply felt desire to achieve the development of something bigger than themselves.

Integrating Threes develop true self-esteem in ways they could never have imagined.

Moreover, through their cooperation with others, both in work and in relationships, they discover in themselves the courage and sense of inner guidance of the healthy Six. This allows them to reveal more of their authentic qualities. Their communication is simple, sincere, and direct; they don't need to amaze people.

No matter how hard Threes work, their pursuit of validation by pursuing non-hearted goals never seems to produce satisfactory results.

To their own surprise, the three find deep satisfaction in the selfless acts they perform and the responsibilities they share as soon as they commit themselves from the bottom of their hearts and thereby develop a true sense of self. They are deeply moved by what they create together with others and see the beauty and goodness of what they have achieved, regardless of whether or not they receive praise for it.

Average Threes tend to consider themselves soloists. They can motivate others and cultivate team spirit, but in the end, they experience themselves as individuals who are alone in the world. Being charged with the role of family hero, support, and comfort were excluded; a hero simply cannot ask too much for help. But when Three to Six integrate, they recognize and accept support in their lives and also dare to ask for help. Usually, such a move in the Three generates an intense fear of failing and disappointing others ("If they know how I really feel, they all let me down"). But if he learns to build solid relationships with selectively selected others, which, as is the case with healthy Sixes, are based on trust and mutual respect,

With attempts to imitate the traits of an average Six, Threes don't make much progress. Exaggeratingly devoting themselves to others and trying to build up their own identity and certainty by establishing links to the left and right will only strengthen their preoccupation with their self-image and performance. On the other hand, as soon as they release their identification with their performance and self-presentation, the faithfulness, intimate dedication, and courage of the healthy Six present themselves in a completely natural way.

Depending on the situation, the associated level of stress, and the development process that the Three has gone through, it can express itself at different levels.

How to Act Proactively as a Three

The keyword is STOP! Allow plenty of time to let emotions rise before you continue to the next task. See your desire to be constantly busy as a way to suppress your fear of emerging feelings. Try to discover your fear of feelings, from which they wish to be constantly busy arises.

Learn to experience the difference between doing and feeling. Recognize when an activity becomes mechanical. Working in a robotic way suppresses your emerging feelings.

Notice when fantasies about success take the place of what you can actually do.

Stay with problems instead of taking a new path, discrediting critics, or explaining failure to be a success. Pay attention to postponing feelings. "I will be happy after the next promotion. After the pay rise, I will have more time. " Notice if you feel you're cheating. "Nobody can look behind my mask. They only see my appearance. "

Experience your unrealistic fear of failure as the workload decreases. Be aware if you make self-evaluation or peer review sessions a task that you want to get to grips with or if you are going to see it as the next job on the agenda.

Learn to recognize feelings. You can start by naming the sensations associated with certain feelings. "My face is warm. My stomach feels tense. " A set time within which self-evaluation takes place reduces the fear of experiencing emotions. Start with thirty minutes and go back to work.

Make choices based on feelings rather than on the status they give you. Allow people to love you for who you are instead of what you do.

2.4 Enneagram Type 4

Type Four is romantic, individualist, melancholic esthete who considers himself or herself special.

The Enneatype Four will strongly recognize itself in this situation:

He is a sensitive person with intensive emotions. He often feels misunderstood and lonely because he feels that he is different from everyone else. His behavior can seem dramatic to others, and he is often blamed for being hypersensitive and inflating his feelings too much. In reality, he internally longs for both an emotional bond and a deep sense of kinship.

He struggles to fully appreciate his current relationships because he tends to want what he cannot get and to despise what he has. The search for an emotional bond is something he has been carrying with him all his life, and the absence of an emotional bond has led to melancholy and depression.

Sometimes he wonders why others seem to have more people than him, better relationships, and happier life. He has a refined sense of aesthetics and experiences a rich world of emotions and meaning.

Further personality traits of the Four

The Four is romantic and imaginative but is solitary and does not interfere too much with others. He is too focused on himself and finds it hard to stand up for himself. Usually, the Four must first process his feeling before he can act, and his habit of being distant annoys people. He is often moody and preoccupied with himself, and, in conflict with others, he usually withdraws. De

Vier is proud of the fact that he is original and resourceful, and people are interested in him because he is calm, unusual, and profound.

Quite often, the Four emphasizes that he is different from his friends and that he is the center of attention; he does not like. When he is worried, he often worries about his problems and is often too emotional and rather undisciplined. He tends to float on his feelings, hold them for a long time, and wants to understand his feelings; he spends a lot of time on introspection.

Fulfilling social obligations is not a high priority for him, and he often feels emotionally too vulnerable to interact with others. Normally pessimistic; the glass is half-empty and cannot get things done because he cannot take advantage of the opportunities offered. He certainly does not do his utmost to meet people and establish relationships. He usually keeps quiet when he sees someone making a mistake because he often has problems with his touch and because he quickly takes everything personally. His friendships often suffer from his personal needs, and intense emotions and events that leave a deep impression are attractive to him. He has the ability to describe inner states of mind and is open and willing to share his feelings with others.

The Four has difficulty coping with his feelings and fears, so it is difficult for him to be strong for others. He usually does what he wants, and in general, he is intuitive and individualistic. He has a need to think about the past and is often restrained from his goal by doubts about himself.

The Basis

In the period from half of the pregnancy to one year after the birth, the essential basic conclusions are determined that form the child to a certain Enneatype. During this period, the child develops his physical identity and fights between 'Trust in' and 'Suspicion of,' a basic bipolar need, or a developmental polarity. This development focuses on the urge for the survival of the individual, and the motor of this urge to survive is the development of fear, whereby experiencing fear leads to a certain action for self-preservation (the conclusion of life). If this action works, this becomes THE solution for the child, and this solution determines the development towards the structure of a certain Enneatype.

Life experiences that shape the Four

The small child was in need when it was forced to focus on things to survive and thereby lost contact with its essence (originality). Experiencing the originality and depth of it and the complete connection with everything.

The painful loss of not being connected to originality gives a terrible feeling of imperfection and a deep, indefinable feeling that something important is missing in life that needs to be recovered.

"Something essential is missing in my life. Others have it. I feel abandoned" is something the Four will often find itself thinking.

Search for the ideal love or circumstances that make you feel loved, whole, and complete. Focus your attention on the intense feeling of circumstances, situations, things, and feelings that you find important and that you miss and try to get them.

They fear being without identity or personal meaning. They feel it is not good to be too functional or too happy, but desire to be themselves, which degenerates into self-indulgence.

It strongly identifies with having feelings of being different and defective and with emotional feelings. Resists recognizing and acknowledging authentic positive qualities in himself and resists the awareness that he is like others.

Sensitive, different, unique, self-aware, soft, intuitive, calm, profound, and honest with oneself.

They try to get hold of the special, ultimate love or situation that makes you complete. For fear of not having an identity or of itself having any personal meaning, Celebrate treats contemptuously, as if others are 'zeros' and have no value or significance.

Emotional passion

Envy, envy, and desire, always looking for what is needed to make life better. Underlying this envy is the feeling of missing something fundamental. Four believe that others possess qualities that they themselves lack. They crave what is missing, but often fail to notice the many blessings in their lives.

They avoid being ordinary and defective, the think nothing should be missing and are fueled by creativity, passion, sympathy, and emotional depth.

They always want what they miss (and emphasize the dissatisfaction with what they already have.

Significant traits

One-on-one relationships: rivalry

Social situations: Shame

Self-preservation: fearlessness (recklessness)

Core beliefs: I am not to love

Defense: introjection, emotional lability

Intuition geared to the best at a distance, within reach the worst

What the Four does not want, avoidances: being ordinary and flawed

Emotional Orientation: envy

Fixation: beauty, the unattainable Work

Motivation: doubt

Common Themes

Looking for a savior, someone who understands him and supports his life and dreams wants to be seen turn into.

Fear abandonment, that nobody will care about him and that he will not get enough support to find and be himself.

Interacts with others by keeping them interested by limiting access to themselves, playing 'hard to get,' and clinging to his supporters.

The four manipulates others by being moody and furious and letting others walk on 'eggshells.'

Core qualities

Pitfall

Allergy

Challenge

Introspection

Navel-gazing

Meaninglessness

Habit

Compassion

Depression

Inaccuracy

Cheerfulness

Sensitivity

Melancholy

Ruthlessness

Business

Passion

Emotionality

Cynicism

Sobriety

The ultimate challenge to grow for the Four is to regain your completeness in the here and now by accepting and appreciating the here and now as it is and accept yourself as you are without the need to be special and unique. Qualities of the essence are the pursuit of the higher idea: the originality and the higher virtue: balance.

Spirituality

According to the spiritual view, the child lost contact with its originality (essence) when it started to focus on things in order to survive. Due to the separation of this original source that connects all living things, Four became melancholy or pleasantly sensitive to the emotions that life is rich with. When envy or envy prevails, emotional equilibrium (balance) turns into despair, as it seems that others enjoy the connectedness denied to Celebrate. The persistence of Vieren in the pursuit of authentic bonding reflects the aspect of the essence that gives all living beings 'one heart'. When the desires that come from envy or envy have been brought back into balance, Celebrates can feel emotionally connected again.

The result

As a child, the Four has tried to 'get the father or mother in' (introjection) from the earliest development and has been disappointed. The child strongly associates itself with father and/or mother; love becomes a pain. A Four often says, "I have no roots" and does not feel strongly connected with life and with itself.

A Four is envious of others who do have this connection. The people who choose to step out of life are often Celebrating. Four always wonders: 'what am I doing here? Is life worth living? De Vier has an intense desire to get to know himself better.

The dilemma

We all know the feeling of envy and envy, the sting that goes through our hearts when we see others enjoying the happiness that we ourselves long for. Celebrates feel misunderstood, while others seem satisfied. Others seem satisfied with their work and their family, while they do not feel seen. Celebrating says it's not a matter of jealousy. They give pleasure to others, but when they see others happy, they are reminded of what they are missing.

Envy and envy motivate them to look for things and status that they assume will make people happy, such as money, a unique lifestyle, expressions of appreciation, and friends.

They do not know that their attention is focused on what they are missing. They only know that it is unbearable to be separated from someone they have a relationship with, that they desperately want to be reunited with the source of love, and that they hate being surrounded by people with less depth but who are the only ones somehow manage to be happy. If they continue to focus their attention in this way, their current relationships seem to offer little in comparison to the promising missing figure.

They become convinced that they have made a mistake and that their happiness must be sought elsewhere. So it feels very natural for them to leave their current situation behind and to resume striving for their distant hope. Four grows by seeing the glass half full instead of half empty. They grow by learning to feel satisfied with what they have.

They have support for loved ones who keep calm during the pull-on / rejection phase, who have an eye for the good things in the here and now, and who stay on the ground with both legs during intensive emotional periods.

The child soul of the Four

Within the dramatic, violent and emotional facade of a Four is a bossy and intrusive little One-child soul who's out to make sure all the little kids behave properly - see to it that none of them get out of step, that their clothes are neat and that they have good manners. This child's soul is a sham, neat, and tidy and full of criticism towards all those who do not follow the rules of the Four. He is a zeal for honesty and accuracy and gets very angry when the other children are naughty. These are the problem children who need to be put on the right track, and in this, we recognize the tendency of the Four to blame others for their problems, as well as their defensiveness in case an "imperfection" is revealed to them.

It is difficult for a Four to recognize this self-inflicted child-soul full of self-esteem, as this feels like his greatest flaw and exposes him to massive attacks and hatred toward himself. Raising awareness of his child's soul instead of letting his aggression implode and focusing on himself, is, in fact, a big part of resolving his inner suffering. The better he sees his child-soul, the better he can see his defensiveness and his need to be right, and if he can acknowledge this, his soul can slowly give up control.

If he understands his need to control others and let them do what he wants, it will become clear how much he lacks in the perception of the perfection of things as they are and, more importantly, of his own perfection. As he increasingly integrates his child-soul, he will see how the purity, radiance, and inherent brilliance of his soul were not allowed or mirrored in his youth. The loss of contact with the Aspect of "Brilliance," which he most strongly embodied, made him feel damaged, and, as a reaction, he developed a personality style based on alienation, abandonment, and desire for connection outside himself.

Every person has the possibility to bring a memory or fantasy to life. The memories can be so strong that they are relived. Such as a beautiful holiday, on a beautiful beach with wonderfully warm weather and nice things that were done with a partner or friends.

Introjection is combining this inner world with the ability to enhance its emotional experience. The strong feelings that accompany this make the memory or fantasy literally and again experienced as real. Because the Romanticist, also called Individualist, tries to avoid everyday life, introjection gives the opportunity to make life more pleasant or interesting with a lot of passion and emotional drama. Individualists, therefore, say that it is not important whether feelings are positive or negative. The only thing that matters is that these feelings are intense. Individualists are, therefore, intense people who can be a challenge for a life partner. If introjection is strong and unconscious, the Individualist can suffer a lot from changing moods. Depressions

The strengths of the Four:

- See the beautiful things.

- Is focused on and has a real eye for beauty.

- I can greatly enjoy small things or incidents.

- It can enjoy melancholy.

- Often has an exceptional image.

- Is a special person.

- Can make substantial contact with people.

- People are looking for this contact of the Four.

- It feels different from others.

- Draw energy from fantasy, artistic activities but also from loss.

- Focuses on what is missing.

- Is emotionally sensitive.

- Feels the mood of others flawlessly.

- Distinguishes itself in the Work through creativity or even genius.

- Is respected by her / his personal vision and ideas.

- Is often aesthetic, refined, and usually knows exactly what it's about.

Tendencies

Fours are inclined to lose themselves in

fantasies about themselves and to turn away from people, both to attract attention and to protect their feelings. To compensate for the problems that inevitably arise with this behavior, the Four takes the step to the Two. After a period of withdrawal and self-absorption, he can thus go to the Two and unknowingly try to solve his interpersonal problems with a somewhat forced kindness, but he is trying too hard. Like Tween, he begins to worry about his relationships and looks for ways to be closer to the people he likes. He needs a lot of reassurance that the relationship is OK. Before that, he regularly and often forces his affection for the other and reminds him or her how meaningful their relationship is.

In more extreme cases, a Four can test through emotional scenes whether others really care for him. This kind of behavior is often debilitating for others and has the consequence that they lose interest in the Four or even abandon him, which naturally triggers the abandonment issues of the latter. The Four can then go to the Two's negative behavior and try to hold the person involved by clinging to him.

They may believe that it is not safe to show the extent of their need and can begin to hide their problems by focusing on other people's problems. (I'm here to help you) The Four can then go to the Two's negative behavior and try to hold the person involved by clinging to him.

In order to be able to continue their unrealistic way of life, as time goes by, it needs more and more emotional and financial support. They fear that without such support, they will no longer be able to realize their dreams. In order to prevent this from exaggerating, stressful people celebrate their importance in the lives of others. They remind the other person how much he or she benefits from his relationship with the Four, take credit for other people's happiness, and look for subtle ways to make people dependent on them. They try to create needs that they can then fulfill themselves and become increasingly jealous and possessive towards the people they care about.

If they have experienced a serious crisis without adequate support or good coping skills, or if they have been chronically abused in their youth, they can pass the 'shock' point and behave according to the unhealthy aspects of their type. This may lead them to the frightening insight that they are destroying their lives and ruining their chances through their fantasizing and emotional self-indulgence. And their fear may be partly justified.

This awareness can be a turning point in the life of the Four. The moment he sees the truth in these fears, he can take the road to health and liberation. On the other hand, he could even try harder to maintain his fantasies and illusions about himself and reject anyone and everything that does not meet his emotional demands. (They are all so cruel and selfish, no one understands me. I know I have to find a job, but I just can't handle it) If the Four perseveres in this attitude, he can fall to unhealthy levels.

At rest or when growing to its performance point, the Four goes to the healthy behavior of the One. Healthy Celebrations act meaningfully in reality. By honoring principles and devoting themselves to activities that go beyond the sphere of their subjective reactions, they discovers not only who they are, but also that who they are is good. They are in direct contact with their instincts and are less enthralled by the emotionally-charged scenarios that they play in their heads. Celebrating that focus on the healthy behavior of the One also realizes that self-expression is not the same as wallowing in one's own moods.

With self-discipline, they work consistently to contribute something worthwhile to their world. They are no longer distant outsiders waiting to be discovered and recognized. They participate fully in life and develop a stronger self-awareness through their Work and through their ties with others. But the Four must ensure that this is not confused with the assumption of the critical or perfectionist traits of the Two. The superego is already punitive enough, and saddling itself with self-improvement projects can easily lead to more self-accusation. It is, therefore, important to develop discernment.

Self-acceptance brings forgiveness for old mistakes and problems. Acceptance of others brings the ability to maintain mutually satisfying relationships.

They recognize in themselves qualities that were previously invisible: power, willpower, determination, and clarity.

Moreover, once it becomes grounded at the moment, all aspects of life become opportunities for creativity. Depending on the situation, the associated level of stress, and the development process that the Four has gone through, it can express itself at different levels.

2.5 Enneagram Type 5

Type Five - the Observer / Researcher / Thinker / Specialist / Expert

He would like to characterize himself as a calm, analytical person who needs more time for himself than most people. He usually prefers to observe what's going on than to interfere. He does not like it when people make a lot of demands on him or when people expect that he knows what he is feeling and then informs them of it. He is better able to come into contact with his feelings when he is alone than with others. He often enjoys his experiences more when he evokes them later than when he actually experiences them. He is almost never bored when he is alone because he has an active spiritual life. He believes it is important to protect his time and energy and therefore, to lead a simple, uncomplicated life and to be as independent as possible.

The Five is generally concentrated and lives intensely. It is difficult for him to stop looking for alternatives and to do something definitive. He is independent, likes to ask difficult questions, is often distant and lost in thought. His interests and hobbies are more important to him than comfort and security. He achieves a lot, despite his lack of interest in developing interpersonal skills.

The Five withdraws more and more as a reaction to the pressure of others and rarely shows its emotions. When the minds are heated, the Five prefers to stay aloof, and he often doubts whether things are what they seem. In discussions with friends, he expresses his own opinion, and he is proud of his clarity and objectivity.

He usually minimizes his feelings and doesn't pay much attention to them. He is willing to give up reward and personal recognition if that means he can do things that he is really interested in. The Five does not have much connection with people and is often so involved with its own projects that it becomes isolated from others.

A large number of his problems are caused by his disinterest in social rules, and he likes to live in his own world. He is contemplative, has a great imagination, and practical results do him less than being able to pursue his personal interests. Before the Five does something, he finds it important to investigate alternatives, and it takes a long time before he takes action.

He often has difficulty falling asleep and often comes across as unusual or even strange. He prefers economy and austerity. He usually sees people as intrusive and demanding and is attracted by topics that others may find disturbing or frightening.

The Basis

In the period from half of the pregnancy to one year after the birth, the essential basic conclusions are determined that form the child to a certain Enneatype. During this period, the child develops his / her physical identity and fights between 'Trust in' and 'Distrust of', a basic bipolar need or a developmental polarity. This development focuses on the urge for the survival of the individual, and the motor of this urge to survive is the development of fear, whereby experiencing fear leads to a certain action for self-preservation (the conclusion of life). If this action works, this becomes THE solution for the child, and this solution determines the development towards the structure of a certain Enneatype.

The little child came in need when he realized that he did not understand something essential to survive.

The feeling of omniscience, just knowing that there is more than a sufficient supply of knowledge and that there is an abundance of energy for everyone.

The world demands too much from the people and gives them too little, which potentially results in a scarcity of money in particular. The world forces itself on me. I need privacy to be able to think and recharge.

Protect yourself against the intrusion of others and their questions and demands by closing off your feelings. If you focus your attention on intruders or get attention from intruders, you close completely. Become autarkic (independent, autonomous, withdraw yourself in yourself), seek privacy and limit your wishes, desires and desires.

Gaining independence and autonomy will free you from the need to need something from others. For fear of being helpless, incapable and incompetent, Vijven makes others feel helpless, incompetent, stupid and incapable.

Emotional passion

Avarice for essential things that are considered to be scarce, such as private time and knowledge. The five believe that they lack inner strengths and that too much interaction with others will lead to catastrophic exhaustion. This passion encourages Vijven to refrain from contact with the world. That way, they can keep their resources to themselves and minimize their needs.

Core qualities

Pitfall

Allergy

Challenge

Sharpness

Arrogance

Stupidity

Simplicity

Independent

Calmness

Exaggeration

Spontaneity

Spirituality

The preoccupation of Fives with mental life reflects the pure knowledge of the essence. This omniscience is a spiritual consciousness that cannot be contained by logical thinking or analysis, and for rationally minded people, it can be a tormenting concept. Spiritual 'knowing' is achieved by concentrating in a specific way and by not attaching ourselves emotionally. This receptive attitude is the opposite of the preceding movement of greed (gluttony) and avarice, which protects them from dependence on others. The task for Fives is to let go of the withdrawn attitude that separates them from the essence so that the many aspects of spiritual knowledge can come into their consciousness.

Desire to reconnect with the life energy and with feelings, especially those of the heart, and realize that there are ample energy and knowledge resources available. Qualities of the essence are the pursuit of the higher idea: omniscience and the higher virtue: non-attachment.

The result

Often the child has a very demanding mother and a father who is often absent. There is a distance between the child and the father. If the father is often away, the child has given up the courage to ask him anything. The child withdraws into its own world and starts thinking about what it feels like.

Another cause may be that there is often a fight between the parents and that the parents show a lot of opposite behaviour. This causes much confusion for the child that the child withdraws.

The formation of the personality of the Five can take place before birth. Then the child already experiences that the mother rejects it. An enormous fear arises, causing the child to freeze his feelings.

The dilemma

In times of scarcity, we put ourselves in the position of Vivien. If we do not have the energy to satisfy our needs, we lower our expectations. In an economy of scarcity, we learn to make ends meet with less: less involvement, less good things and less emotional contact.

Less leads to more: more time, more energy and greater autonomy. Less simplifies everything. Fewer wishes, fewer needs, fewer rules and obligations. If we are freed from some of our emotional burdens and are alone with our thoughts, we, like Fives, will be fed by the silent abundance of our mind.

The house of the Observer looks a lot like a

refuge: little visible, controlled contact and undisturbed time for themselves. The mind becomes a good companion, a friend who sustains him endlessly.

A mind is also a place of refuge that is completely protected against infringement. Fives have no need to share the content of their thoughts. They live in their own minds and can, therefore, provide for their own needs. Observers do not feel deprived unless desires creep in.

In order to live a withdrawn life, a number of physical and emotional conditions must be met. If there is a shortage of this, they will feel a continuing desire to get hold of what is missing. Because autonomy is important to them, they finds it annoying to have needs, and this resentment feeds their desire. It becomes a necessity for them to own that person or those books or that little preciousness that has invaded their loneliness.

Greed is a strong desire to 'own', a wish that is so powerful that it dominates 'non-attachment'. If this habit becomes automatic, their self-observation stops. They find it annoying that they are forced to have feelings. They don't want to have any needs in their lives. They try to let go of their wishes, but they cannot.

Caught between emotional emptiness and the fear of being swallowed by others, they begin to get in touch with their feelings.

Observers grow by connecting their mind with their emotions. They grow by discovering passion in their lives. When they experience the spontaneous flow of emotions and see how they withdraw until they feel empty again, they are free to choose how they want to respond.

Loved ones can help Fives overcome the

fears that arise when they open up emotionally, by not bringing their own emotions into the relationship, by respecting Fives' need for time, privacy and space, by pointing out their tendency to overdo to intellectualize and by creating safe conditions in which the Fives can expose themselves.

The Child Soul of the Five

In every self-contained, withdrawn and silent Five lives a little Eight Child Soul who dreams of being right and eating an infinite amount of ice cream. This child-soul enjoys low and dirty play, fighting out with the other children and immersing himself lustfully in life.

His child's soul can show itself if he curses the other drivers in the privacy of his own car, if he shouts at the referee while watching a football match on television, or if he listens to all politicians for listening to the evening news scammers. The child-soul of a Five can be a small bully and a small fanatic convinced that he is right and not receptive to any other possibility.

He can act defensively and negatively about a perceived weakness and react aggressively if he is doubted. He can be punitive and resentful and want to settle the bill with those who, according to him, has failed him.

For a Five, it can be an ordeal to acknowledge and allow these tendencies of his child-soul, since they represent a strong and enthusiastic relationship with life that comes across as very threatening to him. As a child, his heartfelt and passionate relationship with life was not supported for some reason. His enthusiasm and liveliness, his power and courage, his embodiment of the essential aspect of the 'Power', were tempered. It is quite possible that the rancorous and self-avenging tendencies of his child-soul, when they begin to come to light, are the answer of his soul to this suffocation.

In response to the fact that his "Power" was not allowed, a Five has withdrawn and cut itself off from its own vitality. If a Five allows his voluptuous and dynamic child-soul to surface, he will slowly but surely come back into contact with his liveliness, and he will increasingly feel part of life itself. When he integrates his child-soul, his knowledge becomes more embodied and inclusive, as his heart and belly become involved.

When he makes contact with the courage for a confrontation with the unknown, his life will increasingly become an exciting and attractive adventure in which he immerses himself with heart and soul.

Since his heart and stomach are also

involved. When he makes contact with the courage for a confrontation with the unknown, his life will increasingly become an exciting and attractive adventure in which he immerses himself with heart and soul.

Isolation or letting go (detachment) is a defence mechanism whereby the feelings are released. It is an effective mechanism for temporarily not experiencing emotions, and to be able to respond coldly to a situation.

The feeling experienced by the Observer is one of invulnerability, of not being able to be touched. Because the feeling is released for the purpose of perception and the analysis of what is perceived, interaction with the outside world is primarily rational. There is a continuous interpretation of current and future situations in the form of models, theories and other filters.

These filters and rational explanations for

what is happening in the environment give the Observer a sense of security. What is kept away from consciousness is 'emptiness', or situations that cannot be filtered or explained. Such situations make the Observer restless and give him the feeling of not being prepared for what is to come.

Segmentation is a form of isolation in which the Observer does not let people with whom he or she is in contact get to know each other. Colleagues from work, acquaintances and friends from hobbies or sports and other private environments are unconsciously separated from each other by the Observer. They will not know about each other's existence through the Observer.

This separation gives a sense of certainty to the Observer and contributes to the closedness and sometimes some mystery of this personality type. Insulation, if sustained for too long, will give a feeling of isolation and alienation.

Strength is, at the same time the biggest pitfall. If you use that too much and are not attuned to the other, the other will experience that power negatively and will respond with resistance.

Fives try to cope with stress by narrowing their focus more and more and to withdraw into the safe environment of their heads. If this coping strategy cannot relieve their fear, they can make a move to the Seven. They respond to their isolation by engaging in impulsive activities. They become restless and agitated; their thinking shifts into a higher gear and they compulsively divert themselves from their growing fears. Fearing that they will not find a safe place, they can also fragment their activities. Just like average sevens, they constantly move from one activity to another, from one idea to the next, but they seem unable to find anything that appeals to them.

After they have cut themselves off from their sensual and nurturing needs, they indulge themselves by seeking stimulation and experience in an undifferentiated way. In general, this distraction has little to do with their professional activities. They can go see one movie after another, put it on a drink, get on drugs or plunge into sexual escapades. They can secretly visit all kinds of shady tents, which people who know them never expect to find them there.

Under extreme stress, Fives defend themselves against their fears by becoming aggressive and insensitive in their pursuit of all kinds of desires, and through the use of resources. (Just like less healthy Sevens).

If Fives are under extreme stress for an extended period of time, if they have gone through a serious crisis, without adequate support or coping skills, or if they have been chronically abused in their youth, they can pass the shock point and fall into the unhealthy aspects of their type. This can lead them to the frightening insight that through the projects they have pursued and the way of life that they have created for themselves, they are actually widening their chances of finding a real safe place for themselves. Their fear may then be partly justified.

This awareness can be a turning point. The moment the Five sees the truth in these fears, he can take the road to health and deliverance. On the other hand, however, he could also permanently break all ties with others. He turns his back on the world and isolates himself even more so that he remains free from all offences and can follow his line of thought to a 'logical conclusion'. He gets deeper into his negative, self-destructive spiral of thought ("anyone can walk to

the moon, and nobody will ever hurt me again!")
This seclusion undermines his last bit of
confidence.

If the Five perseveres in this position, he
can make the fall down to unhealthy levels.

Fives realize themselves and stay healthy
by learning to reconnect with their bodies and
instincts, such as integrated Eights. Self-
confidence, the feeling of being full, strong and
capable, is based on the instinctive energy of the
body, rather than in mental structures. Fives grow
by leaving their heads and coming into a deeper
connection with their physicality and vitality.

Greater contact with their bodies releases
enormous fear in the Five. They feel that they lose
their only defence (the head) because of it. For
them, the head is reliable and unassailable, while
they experience the body as weak, vulnerable and
unreliable. Also, through contact with their body,

strong feelings of pain and sorrow about their long isolation can penetrate into their consciousness. Only by being grounded in their bodies can they find support in themselves to deal with these long-suppressed feelings.

If they learn to stay with their instinctive energy, rather than fleeing responsibility by taking distance, Fives participate more fully in their world and apply their knowledge and skills to direct practical problems. They find the strength within themselves to take on major challenges and often take on a leadership role. Others intuitively sense that Fives, devoid of self-interest, are looking for positive solutions. They are therefore happy to support them in projects.

By entering the world, Fives do not lose their mental faculties or expertise that they cultivated during their isolation. Instead, they channel those talents strategically and constructively, such as healthy Eights.

However, they do not get along with attempts to imitate the traits of an average Eight. By focusing on self-protection, releasing themselves from their vulnerability and seeing relationships as confrontations, they do not resolve their emotional detachment and feelings of social isolation.

But when Fives begin to experience and work directly through their identification with the head, the power, the willpower and the self-confidence of the healthy Eight will also develop automatically with them.

Depending on the situation, the associated level of stress and the development process that the Five has gone through, it can express itself at different levels.

2.6 Enneagram Type 6

Type Six - The Loyalist / Doubter / Traditionalist / Faithful / Troubleshooter

He has a lively imagination, especially when it comes to things that could threaten safety and security. He usually recognizes the things that could be dangerous or harmful and then experiences as much fear as when they actually happened. With him, it is always the case that he either avoids danger or goes straight for it. His imagination also leads to his ingenuity and a well-developed, though sometimes somewhat unconventional, sense of humour. He would like life to be a little more secure, but in general, he seems to doubt the people and things around him. He can usually see the shortcomings when someone expresses a point of view. He assumes that as a result, some people find him very astute. He is suspicious about power, and he does not feel very comfortable when people consider his authority. Because he can see what's wrong with a general opinion about certain things, he tends to identify with the fate of the underdog. Once he is committed to something or someone, he is very loyal to that goal or to that person.

The Six is pragmatic and stands with both feet on the floor and is generally easy to hunt for the cupboard. He is not very confident and is generally indecisive and hesitant.

He is usually systematic and careful, and he is stubborn and skeptical. He can trust his friends, and she can trust him. The Six finds comfort and security more important to him than his hobbies, and he is proud of his perseverance and common sense. His duty and responsibility have a lot of meaning for him, and he supports his friends, even though they are wrong.

Problems with others can arise because the

Six can be pessimistic and nagging. He is careful and tries to prepare for unforeseen problems, and he sometimes "tests" his loved ones if they are really there for him. He doesn't like to let go of his obligations from the past, so he has trouble with important changes in life. The Six is proud of its reliability and commitment and generally takes its social obligations very seriously. He soon thinks of the worst, is often hampered by nervousness, uncertainty and doubt and usually has difficulty making decisions.

If he doesn't like someone, he usually shows that in one way or another, but overall he is too cautious and cautious. He has a deep need to "belong" and generally does not have much confidence. The Six often has problems with people because he is evasive and closed, and when he feels insecure, he becomes quarrelsome and defensive. He usually provides a "safety net" to fall back on.

Origins

As a small child it was in need when
confronted with the fear of the parents, and the

[146]

environment was perceived as threatening. The world is dangerous and threatening. People cannot be trusted. Seek safety or, on the contrary, defy safety, avoid danger or, on the contrary, seek danger and dare to cope.

Be alert, alert, questioning or doubtful. Continuously scans the environment for what can go wrong. Search for certainty by either challenging this certainty and defying the danger (contra-phobic style) or look for certainty and avoid all danger (phobic style).

Strongly identifies itself with the need to respond to inner anxiety about an alleged lack of support. Resists acknowledging received support and one's own inner guidance.

Seeking assurance of precisely those things for which there is never enough evidence of certainty. Out of fear of being without support or guidance, Zessen undermines the support systems of others and try to isolate them in one way or another.

Emotional passion

Anxiety associated with all possible dangers, unfortunate coincidences and risks. A more accurate term for this passion is Worry, as anxiety scares us for things that are not actually happening at the moment. Six are constantly worried and worried about possible events in the future.

Significative Traits and Main Themes

Core belief: the world is an unsafe place

Defence: vigilance, questioning, doubtful

Intuition geared to hidden goals of the

other

Six seeks both independence and support. Longs for someone to lean on, but also wants to be 'the strong' himself. Fear of being abandoned and without support, but also of becoming dependent on others.

Interacts with others by being committed and reliable while trying to maintain his independence. Looks for an approach but is also defensive.

Six manipulates others by complaining and by testing other people's dedication to themselves.

Core qualities

Pitfall

Allergy

Challenge

Alertness

Suspicion

Negligence

Leave it

Loyalty

Indecision

Convenience

Self confidence

Spirituality

Six children lost their faith (trust) in others.
As a result, they lost contact with the power and
support of the essence, resulting in a lapse in

doubt and a cowardly assumption of the worst scenario. Falling in fear gives Zessen a lifelong preoccupation with courage and a tendency to look for reliable people and ideals. The Enneagram model, which is about the return to the essence, sees the nine types as searching for those aspects of the virtue that release them from their non-specific suffering. Sixes are consciously or unconsciously inclined to discover faith because they suffer from the lack of it.

The result

The child has always lived in the sense of the world is a dangerous place. The child has had parents who constantly scare children: 'Watch out for this. Watch out for that. Don't play on the street. Don't deal with those people because they aren't good. The parents frightened the child for what could happen. The child has blown that up, and therefore she sees danger behind every tree.

Alternatively, it might be that there is a very strong, dominant, authoritarian father. The child projects that dominance on its environment. That projection is common in a centrophobic Six. It is now not the adult, but the child who projects. The Six forgets that the inner child has been dominated by the highly authoritarian father.

Fear is expressed in two ways: by fighting or fleeing. Sixes who usually flee, want to be protected, such as a man or woman who has a fear of flying. Fighting Sixes (contra-phobic), who are in fact just as scared, will cling to an airplane and undergo the kamikaze mission.

Type Six children responded to adrenaline. They learned to be alert, to question authority and to find out what is really meant. Skeptical and cautious as they are, they look for hidden intentions. Their attention easily changes to the worst-case scenario. Inner doubts are strongest when there is a possibility of taking action. Six have learned to distrust authorities. They find safety in predicting the motives of powerful people before they take the risk of taking action.

It sounds contradictory, but success can be frightening. Becoming visible means being attacked for them. Search for directions for six. "Can you be trusted?" They think in terms of: "What happens if ...? What happens if ...? " If this habit becomes automatic, their self-observation stops. Six are prepared for opposition and doubt whether they will receive support. Because they are flooded by frightening premonitions, they start thinking instead of doing something. Once they start from the worst-case scenario, they cannot possibly act.

Sixes grow by reclaiming faith (trust) in others. They grow by learning to have faith in life.

If they are able to distinguish their fearful thoughts from real danger and if they can see how their increasing hope turns into doubt, they are freed from their preoccupations and are free to choose how they want to respond. They are supported by loved ones who reassure them, who remain unswerving when the future looks doubtful, and who can be trusted by their word.

The Child-soul of the Six

In every Six there is a small lazy man - like a Nine - who just wants to stay under the covers, does not want to go outside, into the world, who just wants to be kept comfortable. For this reason, Sixes are often afraid that if they relax in themselves, they will become inert.

They are afraid they will never be able to

move or take action again, and they are afraid that they will neglect what they have to do in life. This is of course because here, hidden away from consciousness, is this young part, who wants to do nothing but enjoy pleasures and distractions completely. This inner indolence is the real Core of the fear of a Six, he may be more afraid of this tendency in himself than of everything else, and he fears that if he no longer chases himself with his false will, he will lose everything and he will sink into a swamp of laziness. He is afraid that if he makes no effort, nothing will happen and that his life will go wrong.

If a Six allows himself bravely to stop his efforts and leaves himself alone, he may initially experience immobility or a lack of desire to do anything. Over time, the inertia and indolence of his child-soul will transform into what they are an imitation of a loving grasp of the Greater Whole, a feeling that he finds himself in the embrace of the Divine, knowing that he is out of love exists and one is with all existence.

The kindness and benevolence of the universe, the dimension of 'Living Daylight', will become part of his sense of self and the fear in his soul will slowly but surely diminish as he more and more fully realizes his inseparable connection with the Greater Whole. Eventually, his whole attitude of being afraid of others will disappear if he recognizes that his nature is the same as that of all that exists and that the whole feeling of self and the other is an illusion. With the Greater Whole as his inner ground and his perception of its continuity in all its outer forms, he has indeed found the rock on which he can truly stand.

Personality Traits

Projection is the favourite defence

mechanism of the Loyalist. Moreover, it is an important defence mechanism for all Enneatypes, because, with projection, everything that is in the shadow side of human consciousness is projected onto the outside world. It is the principle of the pot that blames the boiler for seeing it black. Everything that people reject in themselves about bad qualities is seen as being done by others. By not judging, but by observing what is happening to yourself, projection can be a tool to improve yourself.

With the Loyalist, the projection will mainly be used to avoid the wrong behaviour. The wrong behaviour can lead to unpleasant and even dangerous situations in the Loyalist's experience. The Loyalist will respond in particular to deviant behaviour and deviant verbal and non-verbal communication from persons in a dominant position.

An example: an employee walks through a corridor and is not seen by a director, who passes by lost in thought without greeting. This employee of the Loyalist type will immediately think: "What is wrong with me?" The deviant non-verbal behaviour of the director is interpreted based on the employee's fears. The Loyalist thinks he can deduce what this director thinks about him. The problem, however, is that one can never do this with 100 per cent certainty, it keeps on guessing.

An extreme case was a marketing manager who, objectively speaking, received a logical and deserved promotion. But she was convinced that she had been promoted and that she would have to fail in her new position.

The focus on 'right' behaviour eventually leads to rigid behaviour. This will also lead to a limitation of the expressive possibilities of the

Loyalist. A Loyalist described how in social contacts, she always tried to estimate how people looked at her. If she met someone who might have had a better education, she would look up to this person and "talk up." If she had the idea that a conversation partner had a lesser education, she would look down on it and talk from above. By maintaining this behaviour for a long time, a Loyalist will increasingly restrain himself mentally and emotionally.

Response to stress

Six are investing their time and energy tirelessly in 'security systems'. When the stress exceeds their normal ability to cope, they can make the step to the Three, making them even more driven and potentially work-addicted. Sixes out of three become stronger image-conscious; they develop the right appearance (clothing, hairstyle), the right gestures, the right jargon and the right attitude to be acceptable in their circle. In this way, they hope to take on people and avoid rejection.

However, others feel that their "kindness or professionalism" has forced something, which makes them wonder what the Six actually carries in its shield. Like Three, Sixes can become competitive, albeit usually through identification with particular groups or beliefs (a favourite sports club, their business, a lifestyle, school, nationality or religion). They can also become smart and promote themselves. They adopt a condescending attitude, disqualify others and boast of their own superiority in a desperate attempt to defend themselves against their low self-esteem and feelings of inferiority.

If Sixes are under extreme stress for an extended period of time, or if they have experienced a serious crisis without adequate support or coping skills, or if they have been chronically abused in their youth, they can pass the shock point and fall down to the unhealthy aspects of their type. This may lead them to the frightening insight that their own combative acts or defensive reactions actually harm their certainty. And their fear may be partly justified.

This realization can mark a turning point in the life of the Six if he sees the truth in these fears he can take the road to health and liberation. On the other hand, he may also become more panicked and more reactive: "I will do everything for you, do not leave me" or at the other extreme: "It will repent that they have exploited and thwarted me!" If The Six perseveres in this position, he can make the fall down to the unhealthy levels. If you notice that you or someone you know shows the warning signs (see warning signs) for a longer period of time (longer than a few weeks), then it is highly recommended that you go into therapy or call in other help.

Integration

The fearful, pessimistic Six relaxes more and becomes more optimistic, like healthy Nines.

Sixes realize themselves and remain healthy by, like healthy Nines, becoming balanced in their instincts and grounding in their bodies. To find the desired stability, they must ground and focus on the here and now. Many Sixes are active, even sporty, but that is not the same as being in contact with the body's experiences and feelings from moment to moment. As a counterbalance to their non-stop thinking, they could focus their attention on their sensory impressions, so that they get something else to identify with themselves than just their head.

If Sixes start to inhabit their bodies more fully, this can be accompanied by feelings of panic and anxiety, certainly when there is a background of abuse or abuse. They can vibrate. At those moments, it is important that they realize that through these reactions, the body processes old fears and pains and not that they are indications of the danger of being in the here and now. As they can become more aware of their fear, without reacting to it (containment), they open themselves more and more confidently to life.

However, by imitating the traits of average Nines, Sixes will not find this stability. Self-complacency, surrender, or fall into comforting, ingrained routines, only reinforces their tendency to cling to people and activities anxiously for certainty. Forced attempts to take things easily or to remain passive do not put an end to their deeper anxiety and can only increase their psychic witch's cauldron.

But as they become more skilled at staying with themselves without responding to their fears, they feel more and more supported, not only by important others or their work but by existence. They realize that life is good and they are positive, and they know that everything will be fine. This is not based on a belief or some trick of the mind, but on a calm and stable inner knowing that requires no explanation or external support.

From this position of justified openness, Sixes are aware of their ties and what they have in common with humanity. They embrace and accept others, regardless of whether their opinions or way of life are familiar. They are brave through and through and not from a counter-phobic reaction to fear, but in and out of themselves, from their Core.

Their courage comes from a sense of true

inner solidarity and deep connection with themselves and everything that lives. Because of this, integrating Sixes, just like healthy Nines, are able to take on big challenges within themselves, evenly and evenly, and even endure tragedies or threats.

Depending on the situation, the associated level of stress and the development process that the Six has gone through, it can express itself at different levels.

2.7 Enneagram Type 7

Type Seven - the bon vivant / adventurer / planner / pleasure seeker / dreamer / optimist.

He is an optimistic person who likes to come up with new and interesting things. He has a very active mind that quickly jumps back and forth between different ideas. He likes to have an overall picture of how those ideas fit together, and he becomes very enthusiastic if he can connect concepts that, at first seemed to have nothing in common. He finds it difficult to stay busy with thankless and recurring tasks. He likes to be involved in the start of a project, at the planning stage, when a large number of interesting options still have to be chosen. When he is no longer interested in something, he finds it difficult to stay focused on it because he wants to continue with what has once again aroused his interest. If there is something unpleasant, he would rather focus his attention on nicer ideas. He believes that people are entitled to a pleasant life.

The Seven is generally spontaneous and likes to have fun, and when a new experience occurs, he usually wonders if it's fun. He is downright, often says what others dare not say and is usually adventurous and willing to take risks. He is often afraid that he is missing something that is even better or more fun, and when he is worried, he often spoils himself with something nice. De Zeven is usually outgoing, and he and a social person are appreciated for his zest for life and sense of humour. In response to pressure from others, he becomes more aggressive and dealing with details is not his strong point.

If he has concerns, he likes to seek distraction for himself, and he is spontaneous and improvises when there are problems. One of his greatest strengths is to come up with new ideas and make people enthusiastic about them. He tries to keep his life fast, intense and exciting and is too easy and too indulgent to himself. He has a fast mind and unbridled energy and does not have much self-discipline. In a first meeting, he is pleasant and entertaining, and he is usually quickly excited, a quick talker and a wit. He doesn't get things done because he sees too many possibilities, and when he has doubts, he tries different things to see what he likes best. On the whole, he is rash, with superficial feelings.

It generally likes to have things celebrated, pushes its limits, is happy with its enthusiasm and is open to new experiences. He tends to exaggerate and run too fast, and strong mood swings are typical of him. He usually anticipates the things he is going to do, and if he has to choose between something familiar and something new, he chooses something new. He often worries that he does not have the self-discipline to focus on what really satisfies him.

One of the biggest problems with the Seven is to take back gas, and he usually follows his feelings and impulses. He does his utmost not to be seen as boring.

Significant Traits

The world limits and frustrates people and

causes pain that can be escaped. Life offers numerous opportunities and options. I look forward to the future.

Life conclusion for self-preservation, the coping strategy of the Seven:

Plan as many enjoyable, positive options as possible. Introduce yourself and engage with interesting activities and experiences. Focus your attention on multiple options, occasions and opportunities.

The desire to be happy often degenerates into hectic escapism.

Seven strongly identify with the state of excitement they find themselves in by anticipating positive experiences in the future. They resist recognizing and acknowledging personal pain and anxiety ,try to keep life positive and idealistic and continue to believe that suffering can be avoided. Out of fear of suffering helplessly and being short of something, Sevens hurt others and make them feel that they are short of something.

Emotional Passion

Gluttony for interesting ideas and pleasant experiences, both in the present and in the future. This mainly concerns the insatiable desire to 'cram full' with experiences. Sevens try to overcome feelings of inner emptiness by embarking on a range of positive, stimulating ideas and activities, but they never think they have enough.

Other Significant Traits

Core belief: I am empty

Defense: pleasure, positivity

Emotional Orientation: immaturity

Fixations: making plans

Motivation: entrepreneurship

Emphasizes positive experiences, joy, activity, excitement and pleasure.

Avoids seeing his own pain and emptiness; his role in others and self-inflicted suffering.

Manipulates others by confusing them and imposing its own demands on them.

Distinctive Aspects:

Dullness

Thoughtfulness

Charm

Narcissism

Confinement

Curiosity

Restlessness

Predictability

Thoroughness

Spirituality

Work is a commonly used concept that stands for the way of focusing attention that goes beyond our personality or 'false' self. Spiritual work depends on the ability to look within and to distinguish between the outer and the inner reality. When the mind becomes fascinated by the glories of material life, working on a spiritual level degenerates into pleasing planning and an excessive need for life experiences. Sobriety, the positive counterpart of immaturity, is another commonly used concept that refers to the spiritual development of the Seven through concentration, limitation, and dedication.

The Result

With a Seven, there is often talk of a stuck marriage of the parents. There may also be a distant, low-emotional mother, which the child experiences as a burden. It then shows the reaction: away from my parents' situation. Then you get the opposite: approaching nice things and away from the annoying.

The Dilemma

Sevens have learned to charm and disarm;

they focus on pleasure and avoid the pain. Their escape route is a stream of positive choices, ideas and visions for the future. When they encounter difficulties, attention shifts and reserve plans are deployed. Sevens are fascinated by pleasant experiences, a promising future and stimulating ideas. They feel committed to an attractive and adventurous life and are the optimists of the Enneagram.

Everything is fine when they have good times ahead. Life is okay when the energy starts to flow.

Irregularity is a feast of experiences. Make the weekly schedule even fuller and fill the mind with plans. Disappointments hardly come to the surface. Other options seem attractive. Suddenly there is a whole new idea. Sevens pursue their own interests, supported by a sense of self-worth.

They go to places where they are welcome

and are attracted to people who appreciate them. Supported by feelings of self-worth, they go through life without being aware of the pain of others. For Sevens, people are fascinating, and every day brings its own experiences. Their attention is focused on the next event and life goes on.

If positive labelling becomes automatic, their self-observation stops. They do not realize that they only think positively. They confuse possibilities and facts. They only know that it annoys them when others tell them what to do. That boundaries are the result of petty thinking. That rules are bothersome and probably unimportant, and that it is 'killing' if their options diminish.

Sevens grow by 'staying' instead of leaving. They continue to learn to cope with pain. When they see how their attention drops when they get connected to something, they are free to choose how they want to respond. They do well to stay another minute instead of leaving.

They are supported by loved ones who accept both pleasure and pain in the relationship, who recognize the needs and value of friends, who see when their interests start to spread and who create a framework within which emotional depth can occur.

The Child Soul of the Seven

In every seemingly generous and carefree Seven, there is a very stingy, refused, and withdrawn child-soul, a little Five. He stubbornly holds on to what he has and puts away all his sweets and toys so that the other children cannot reach it and take it away from him. Driven by the fear of loss and an inner feeling of scarcity, he feels empty inside and anxious that food will no longer come his way.

Despite all apparent coziness, optimism and interest in the life of a Seven, this young place on the inside wants to hide from life and be connected to it remotely. This child soul can also be a little "nerd" and a know-it-all who rely primarily on his intellect. It is likely that in the youth of a Seven his tendency to isolate himself, to be locked in and to be alone was not allowed and that he received the message that he should focus more on the outside world and be cheerful. It is also likely that his mental faculties were supported and developed at the expense of a more inner and intuitive understanding, making him a little intellectual who felt separated from the other children.

Because of the need for a Seven to be cheerful, optimistic and enthusiastic about things, it is very difficult for him to acknowledge this reclusive, frightened and recluse-like young part of himself. What feels the most difficult is the feeling of scarcity that drives his child's soul, the dry, inner emptiness and dryness, and in the first instance a Seven experiences it as threatening to make contact with this. The abler he is not to condemn and reject this part of himself, the more the tendency to covet and isolation will transform, especially if his sense that he is ultimately a separate entity, and thus someone cut off from the remainder of existence.

When his sense of separateness from Totality and others is addressed, and his inner desert flourishes with all the flowers of Essence, his soul will really know immediately. He will feel part of the whole and understand from his own experience that being separate is impossible, and being 'okay' will be real rather than reactive.

Response to Stress

Under increased stress, Sevens realize that they need to focus their energies if they want to achieve things. Just like the average ones, they restrain themselves. They are going to work harder, believing that only they can do the job properly. And they try to keep their behavior under control. They force themselves to continue with what they started with, but nevertheless quickly become annoyed by these structures and boundaries. They can then become even more restless and distracted, or they control themselves even more and become inflexible. In that case, their usual exuberance gives way to grim seriousness.

Just like the average ones, Sevens try to

teach others under stress. Whether it is an exciting book or an exciting workshop, or a good supermarket, or a certain political or spiritual point of view, their enthusiasm for their own opinions can quickly turn into an urge to enter into discussions or to criticize other people's views.

They can become curt and impersonal and are annoyed by any kind of incompetence, both with themselves and with others. Under great stress, their underlying anger and resentment bubble to the surface and cool their frustration in swearing guns, jail and sarcastic remarks.

If Sevens are under extreme stress for an extended period of time, or if they have been through severe crises without adequate support or coping skills, or if they have been chronically abused in their youth, they can pass the shock and fall to the unhealthy aspects of their type.

This may lead them to the frightening insight that they are no longer in control of their lives and that their choices and actions actually only aggravate their pain. Their fear may then be partly justified.

This awareness can be a turning point in the life of a Seven. The moment he sees the truth in these fears, he can take the road to health and liberation. On the other hand, however, the Seven could become even more fragmented, impulsive and manic, plunging into reckless activities in order to evade its pain at all costs.

If the Seven perseveres in this position, he can make the fall down to the unhealthy levels. If you notice that you or someone you know shows the warning signs (see warning signs) for a longer period of time (longer than a few weeks), then it is highly recommended that you go into therapy or call in other help.

Sevens realize themselves and stay healthy by learning to taking it slower and to calm down their constant, rapid mental activity, so that their impressions can touch them deeper, in the way of healthy Fives. This not only promotes their productivity and creativity, but they also find more of the guidance they are looking for. Moreover, what they produce possesses much more resonance and meaning for others.

Cultivating a calmer, more focused mind brings Sevens into closer contact with their own essential guidance. This allows them to determine better which experiences will really be of value to them — no longer distracted by their fear of making the wrong choices and missing out on something that may be more exciting, integrating Sevens know what to do without a hint of doubt. Exploring reality with greater depth does not have to cause them to lose their spontaneity or enthusiasm; on the contrary, they become freer to assimilate fully within themselves at any moment.

However, integrating Sevens do not get along with imitating the qualities of average Fives. Getting lost in thought, emotional detachment and fear of the needs of others will only make their cerebral circus worse. Trying to force oneself to concentrate will not do anything either, because such attempts are based on repression. But as Sevens learn to calm their minds and tolerate the rising fear, they will gradually and naturally develop the clarity, the innovative capacities, the insight and the knowing qualities of the healthy Five.

Type Eight - The Boss / Warrior / Assertive / Leader / Protector / Breadwinner

He approaches things in an all-or-nothing way, especially when it comes to topics that affect him. He attaches great importance to being strong, honest and reliable. You know what you can do with him. He only trusts others when they have proven that they are reliable and he likes when people are direct. He feels when someone is insincere, lies or tries to manipulate him. He finds it hard to tolerate people's weaknesses unless he understands the reason for their weakness or sees them trying to do something about it. He also finds it difficult to follow orders or instructions if he does not respect the authorized person or does not agree with him. He would rather take the lead himself. When he is angry, he can hardly hide his feelings.

He confronts when needed, and he is smart. Others count on his strength and decisiveness, he is brutal and dominant, and he likes to be a mainstay for others. He is afraid that someone will abuse him if he drops his shield, and he likes to challenge people, "shake them up."

If he has a conflict with others, he fights it out, and he is very strong and assertive. He motivates people by making big plans and making promises.

When things get hot, he wants to get involved, and problems arise with others because he is bossy and takes the lead. Independence and independence are important to him, and one of his strongest points is making sure that things get done and arranging the means for this. He gives many people a goal and motivation. It does not spend much time on introspection; getting things done is more important to him. He prefers to take the lead, and people trust him because he is trustworthy and takes care of them.

He likes to let the world know that he exists and rarely has trouble making decisions. He is usually well-considered, straightforward and thoughtful, but when angry, he gives someone a scolding. A strong point is his ability to take the lead on problems, and his approach is to show people how they can help themselves. He enjoys difficult situations or works under high pressure and is practical and expects his work to yield concrete results. He often repels people because he is too aggressive and in disagreement, he is often crude and direct.

He must be strong for others, so he doesn't have time to deal with his feelings and fears.

The Basis

In the period from half of the pregnancy to one year after the birth, the essential basic conclusions are determined that form the child to a certain Enneatype. During this period, the child develops his physical identity and fights between 'Trust in' and 'Suspicion of', a basic bipolar need or a developmental polarity.

This development focuses on the urge for the survival of the individual, and the motor of this urge to survive is the development of fear, whereby experiencing fear leads to a certain action for self-preservation (the conclusion of life). If this action works, this becomes THE solution for the child, and this solution determines the development towards the structure of a certain Enneatype.

He desires to become strong and powerful to earn respect. Introduce others to your personal will and truth. If necessary, use anger and become confrontational. Deny personal vulnerability. Focus attention on personal strength, control and injustice.

He fears being harmed or controlled by others.

He needs winning protection and domination through strength and invulnerability. Out of fear of being harmed or controlled by others themselves, Eights, through their combative and intimidating threats, make others afraid that they will be harmed or controlled.

Emotional Passion:

Lust for life, lust, lust and excess. The powerful energy that makes the Eight shine. This passion is not just about sexual desire. Eights are 'pleasurable' in the sense that they are driven by a constant need for intensity, control and self-expansion. Lusts encourage Eights to try to push through everything in their lives, to assert their will.

Core belief: I have no control

Defence: denial, insensitivity

Intuition tailored to control

Avoidances: weakness, vulnerability, powerlessness

Emotional Orientation: lust / zest for life / lust / excessiveness

Fixations: power and revenge Work

He seeks independence and independence. If others want as little as possible, they want to be themselves. Fears to be controlled or dominated by others. Is, therefore, afraid of intimacy and that he becomes vulnerable through too much trust or too much compassion. Interacts with others by staying on guard, not allowing others to get too close and suppressing pain and the needs of others.

Eights manipulate others by dominating them and demanding that they do what they says.

Core qualities

Provocation

Cowardice

Flexibility

Immediateness

Boldness

Sanctity

Tact

Courage

Authority

Arrogance

Flattery

Spirituality

The preoccupation of Eights with justice points to the search for truth. If pure truth prevailed, control would be superfluous. According to the spiritual view, children are innocent who saw that the truth could be distorted and betray the innocence. Eights immediately realized that the strong dominate the weak, that vulnerability is seen as a weakness, and that the good things in life end up with those in control. This inevitable confrontation nurtured their feelings of revenge and mobilized their strength, energy and lust (excess) to satisfy their personal needs.

The Result

Often at a very young age, the child has the feeling of being terribly humiliated (sometimes there is violence) and, in his eyes, he has incredible collisions with the father or the father figure. In a number of cases, such a child is often humiliated and beaten. It makes the decision: once but never again and immediately builds an armor around it.

Many of these children are hyperactive and often hear that they are 'difficult to raise'. It is difficult to give these children rules in such a family context; the child often discovers these rules outside the family. For example, it teaches at the sports club to curb its aggression.

The Dilemma

If we are completely certain of the truth and act accordingly, we will move into the position of the Eight. Enormous power and determination come to us, which we cannot hide. Our mind stops doubting. Emotions are pushed aside in the impulse of action. Even before we know what we are going to do, we move, and before we know what we want to say, we hear ourselves talking. This is not about being brave; we cannot be reticent when the truth is at stake, even if we want to.

Because power commands respect, Eights learn to keep their feelings under control. They cannot be vulnerable and invincible at the same time. They cannot be concerned about the needs of others, while others seem inclined to deny their needs. They cannot allow tenderness, fear or regret when they are in combat formation. The primary goal is to gain control over the territory and be the first to be there.

If the topdown approach works well, Eights can forget their degree of influence on others. If the 'strongest win' approach works well, they don't have to look at how their behaviour affects others. They are only aware of their own needs and will use everything they have at their disposal to fulfil their needs. They forget to consult, inform whether an agreement can be reached and do not realize that they are busy putting their own agenda forward.

They only know that they think it is terrible to be disadvantaged, that disapproval of their behaviour sounds ridiculous, and that obstacles are a marginal phenomenon.

When they think they are disadvantaged, their energy comes on. Energy leads to speed, smartness and strengthens their own will. If this habit becomes automatic, their self-observation stops. The results of their struggle become predictable. If they have won the 'war', they will be the only ones left on the battlefield.

Eights grow as they explore their ideas about justice, hear the other side of the story, and learn to wait. If they feel confident enough to moderate their own position and realize that escalating situations is a way for them to gain control, they are freed from their preoccupation and are free to choose how they want to respond.

The Child Soul of the Eight

In the harsh and no-nonsense eight, who enjoys measuring his guts with that of others, controlling and control life and to triumph over every adversity, there is a needy, affectionate and lonely little Two-child- a soul that desperately wants to be loved and held.

The child-soul of an Eight wants to crawl against others, as close as possible and can be quite persistent and demanding. Under the power of an Eight, this child-soul is full of all sorts of emotions that he believes are weak, as others need, are afraid of rejection, uncertainty and a deep sense of sadness and loneliness. From the feeling that his contact and loving qualities as a child were undesirable, an Eight responded by essentially saying "rotten" to everyone he felt dependent on and proving he didn't need anyone.

What he felt as his vulnerable, soft gut feelings, he hid under a varnish of numbness, and in the course of the process, he closed his openness and susceptibility.

When the Eight comes into contact with the defensiveness behind its pride and the sense of rejection and neediness that underlies it, it can feel as if its entire world is collapsing. He has made every effort not to experience the 'weak' spots in his soul and often has the feeling that he will not survive if he lets them appear. If he lets himself come into contact with his need and pain, his heart can open again, and his soul becomes transparent.

He can be hit again, and if he comes into contact with reality with less and less thick and armored skin, he will slowly but surely start to feel more connected to life. Instead of trying to wrest life away from what he needs, he will discover that his soul relaxes, melts and merges with its essential nature, the honey-like nectar of which fills its soul in the form of "Melting Love."

Instead of fighting with reality, he will be

united with it; and as he surrenders more and more fully to the Total Being, he will find, instead of the capitulation that he feared, fulfilment and loving union.

Response to stress:

If tensions rise, Eights can only partially implement their specific methods for dealing with problems. Ultimately, their self-assertive, confrontational attitude confronts them with challenges they no longer feel comfortable with. When they have taken too much hay, they can take the step to negative behavior from the Five, avoiding conflicts to draw up strategic plans, gain time and gather their strengths.

Eights can become solitary figures in such periods. They spend many hours worrying, reading and gathering information so that they are better able to assess the situation. They demand the time and privacy to sort things out before they can take action again. They can lose a lot in their plans and projects. They work late into the night while avoiding others and covertly about their activities. They can also seem peculiarly calm and distant, which often comes as a surprise to those who are used to their more assertive, passionate qualities. Furthermore, during periods of stress, Eights can become nervous, tend to minimize their comfort and needs and tend to take care of themselves poorly. Insomnia and unhealthy food regimens are not uncommon.

Feelings of rejection can drive Eights to some dark aspects of the Five. They can be terribly cynical and late-thinking about the beliefs and values of others.

If Eights have experienced a serious crisis

without adequate support or good coping skills, or if they have been chronically abused in their youth, they can pass the 'shock' point and behave according to the unhealthy aspects of their type. This may lead them to the frightening realization that their rebellious reactions and attempts to control others actually only put them at greater risk, so they are less safe, no longer.

This can, in turn, lead to the fear that others, including their trusted loved ones, will actually leave them or perhaps even turn against them. And their fear may be partly justified.

This awareness, though frightening, can mark a turning point in the life of the Eight. The moment he sees the truth in these fears, he can take the road to health and liberation.

On the other hand, he can become more combative, rebellious and threatening and desperately try to control everything at all costs.

(It is I against the world. Don't let anyone even think of thwarting me; I will crush them in front of them.) If the Eight perseveres in this position, he can make the fall down to unhealthy levels. If you notice that you or someone you know shows the warning signs (see warning signs) for a longer period of time (longer than a few weeks), then it is highly recommended that you go into therapy or call in other help.

To children and animals, they can lower their cover and allow their own softness. But if Eights want to embrace their own generosity, they will first have to have the courage to come into contact with it. This requires that they have faith in something beyond their own ingenuity and power and that in turn requires that they release many of their fundamental natural defenses. It is important for the Eight to realize that he does not get along with imitating the qualities of the Two. By flattering others and trying to make them happy in a forced way, they do not yet open their hearts; moreover, others will often realize that it is insincere.

Integrated Eights are excellent leaders because they show their deep respect and appreciation for other people in a clear way. They are also effective because they have a clear sense of limits and limits. By learning to love themselves and accepting vulnerability in their lives, their health and well-being improve. They work hard, but also know when it's time to rest, eat and refuel. Instead of indulging in excesses or seeking more intensity, they opt for leisure activities that are really beneficial to them.

Self-Help

Give others the opportunity to take the initiative. Learn to wait and listen to what is going on before you respond. Note when your sense of insecurity increases and you tend to escalate things, stir up disagreements, let things fall apart or polarize in a conversation. Recognize boredom or disinterest as a possible "mask" for feelings of weakness.

Observe that the behavior of others can be just as appropriate and logical as your own reaction. Discover the points of agreement in different points of view. See that confrontation and physical excess can cover your real feelings. See that the emergence of real feelings can be accompanied by depression. Label your 'weaker' feelings as a sign of progress.

Realize that a preoccupation with justice, protection and control often divides others into camps of "friends" and "enemies." Remember to write down insights. Fight it stubbornly. Read the insights once in a while to combat denial.

Learn to control anger. Both suppressing and expressing anger can have negative consequences. Learn to see that concluding a compromise does not mean 'giving up'.

2.9 Enneagram Type 9

Type Nine - the Mediator / Healer / Reconciler / Comforter / Optimist / Utopist

He seems to have the ability to oversee all points of view easily. Sometimes he can even seem indecisive because he can see the advantages and disadvantages of everything. Because he has the ability to see all sides of a case, he can often help people to resolve their differences. This same ability means that he sometimes takes more account of the position, agenda and personal preferences of others than of his own. When that happens, his attention often diverts to trivial, trivial tasks. He finds it hard to know what is really important to him, and he avoids conflict by doing what others want. People often find him laconic, engaging and accommodating. A lot has to happen before he shows his anger directly to someone. He likes a comfortable, harmonious and pleasant life.

Further personality traits of the Nine:

He has a tendency to avoid confrontations and is generally difficult to chase. He tends to focus too much on others and often has problems with others because he does not want to get involved too much. He likes to keep his balance and peace of mind and can easily distance himself from problems when they arise. Usually too shy to show his skills. He gives in too easily, is most accommodating and lenient, and harmony and tolerance are important to him.

Very often, the Nine emphasizes how much he has in common with his friends. He would rather not respond to his feelings for fear that this would lead to more problems and try to keep his life regular, stable and peaceful. He is modest and happy if he can keep his pace. He sees himself as sunny and informal and usually easily lets someone else take the lead. Normally he is optimistic, the glass is half full, and most of the time he thinks that everything will end up on his feet. He does not stand up for himself enough and is committed too much to have everything in order for others.

Overall, the Nine is balanced, "still waters have deep grounds", but often it is too open and trusting. He would rather avoid difficult situations or work under high pressure, so he will not put others under pressure. He likes situations that give him a calm feeling, in which he can feel at ease.

He probably finds himself too passive and unconcerned and prefers not to dwell on disturbing or frightening subjects for too long. In the event of a serious setback, he feels discouraged and suffering, and one of his biggest problems is getting rid of his temper. He often wonders why people focus on the negative while there is so much beauty in life.

The Basis

The little child came into distress when it became indolent or neglectful of the essential consciousness of unconditional love, of pure being.

Knowing the unconditional love, making everyone equally important, everyone equal and making everyone respect.

The world makes you unimportant and / or demands that you lose yourself in it. My efforts will yield nothing. Do not cause difficulties. Keep the peace.

Forget yourself and find where you belong. Make your own personal priorities, subordinate to external requirements and priorities.

Distinctive Traits

Strongly identifies with the sense of inner stability that he experiences by distancing himself from intense impulses and feelings. Resists recognizing and acknowledging one's own strengths and capacities.

Peaceful, relaxed, resistant, stable, meek, natural, laid back and friendly.

For fear of breaking contact with others themselves, by ignoring them, Nines give others the feeling that they are breaking contact with Nine.

Emotional Passion:

An inert lock on yourself, which expresses itself as laziness. The energy goes to other people and many replacements for your own priorities.

Laziness is not simply laziness because Nines can be fairly active and competent. Rather, it is about a desire not to let yourself be touched by life, a reluctance to plunge into a life full and vital.

Core belief: it happened to me

Defense: self- a sedation

Avoidance: conflicts

Emotional Orientation: laziness

Fixations: self-neglect

motivation: harmony / impulses

He emphasizes the positive qualities of others and their environment. Idealizes his world. Avoids seeing the problems with his loved ones or environment and his own lack of development. Problems with needs by feeling overwhelmed by their own and other people's needs; does not want to tackle either.

Nine manipulates others by leaving and by resisting others passively-aggressively.

Core qualities

Avoiding conflict

Unapproachability

Struggle

Admissibility

Imbalance

Slowness

Indecision

Spirituality

Babies 'are' the essence, in the sense that their consciousness is permeated with unconditional love, which is inherent in being pure. When the personality started to form in the first years of life, they became indolent or neglected with regard to their spiritual nature. Laziness is an exaggerated adaptation, a desire to live pleasantly and mechanically instead of being decisive with regard to the essential aspects of life. Nines avoid conflict and are absorbed in the agenda of others, which is an imitation of the love that unites all creatures.

The Result

Children who develop according to the Nine structure are often or:

Model children who have been overlooked. For example, if you are the fourth child in a family, they think you can do it all yourself. Because the child is overlooked, it suppresses its feelings.

Alternatively, the child stands between two parents who have a conflict with each other. The child cannot choose between his father and mother. It withdraws, falls asleep and is no longer aware of the outside world. Nines often turn out to have difficulty making decisions later.

Nines need to reclaim unconditional love for themselves, passing this love on to others.

The Dilemma

At times when we feel inseparable, we put ourselves in the perspective of the Nine. Borders fade away when someone else's life becomes the motive for our own life. Once we are absorbed in the other, it feels like one skin and one person. We put our energy on the agenda of our companions. Their interests become essential; their opinion seems plausible. We feel excited about their lives, which have become the center of our own lives.

A tension arises between wanting to settle for love and defending their independence. The question is, "Do I agree and follow, or do I not agree and cause a conflict?" Accepting it feels like giving in, but it is hard to say no. They are absorbed in someone's life, so choosing no longer matters. They can more easily see the value of the position of others than the value of their own position. Laziness means 'adopting a lazy attitude to life'. Decisions are difficult when conflicting opinions all seem to be equally valuable. Their attention is shifting from the central problem to secondary issues. They end up on a sidetrack of chores and backlogs. Their energy is distracted from their essential daily task. Their pace is slowing. Without realizing it, a pattern of retention develops. The energy that is intended for primary goals is transferred to secondary goals.

Nines grow if they pay attention if they structure their own agenda and keep following the trail. If they can see how they adopt a new position, they are freed from their preoccupation and are free to choose how they want to respond. They can learn to separate themselves from others and to pay attention to themselves. They are supported by loved ones who help them to pursue personal goals, who keep confirming their progress, and who remind them of their deeply cherished goals, which can only be achieved by making their own choices.

The Child Soul of the Nine

The centre point of the Nine is point Three

[217]

so that the child-soul of a Nine initially appears as a tendency to cheat and lie in order to show the other what approval will reap. In addition to the Passion of lying, there is a young place in every Nine that wants to be seen, to shine and to be the centre of attention. So there is a little guy who wants to do his dance and get applause. Behind the tendency for self-denial of a Nine lies a drive and often a ruthlessness to succeed, usually well hidden and banished from consciousness. Nines are often afraid that they appear too intrusive and take up too much space, which is the shadow of their child-soul that falls over their consciousness.

If a Nine allows himself to come into contact with this structure within himself and its qualities, he will increasingly experience himself as a complete person. The exhibitionistic tendencies will transform into a genuine recognition of his person. He will see that in his youth, he was not supported to be a self-employed person, and thus he became compliant and denied himself to get approval. By finding himself back as personally valuable and loving, he will be led to the realization of himself as a personal embodiment of Totality, "the Pearl of Inestimable Value," a radiant and luminous presence that is independent of the limitations of his conditionings.

All Enneatypes have a favorite defense mechanism, but you could say that the Peacekeeper has no favorite defense mechanism. Defense mechanisms such as negation and identification enable a person to block things directly from consciousness. You experience something that you absolutely do not want to experience, and negation or identification allows you to keep this experience out of consciousness effectively. However, to keep a nasty experience out of his consciousness, the Peacekeeper must engage his entire consciousness into a completely different experience. This is called anesthesia. Anesthesia can be obtained through television, by eating, by sex, by computer games a. The Peacekeeper thinks he can avoid a nasty experience by being completely absorbed in these secondary activities. The problem is that he forgets himself.

What a Peacekeeper tries to avoid with anaesthesia are conflicts. This will lead to conflict-avoiding behaviour and a non-assertive attitude. Although the Peacekeeper may seem very nice because of this, it will not be effective in the long run. Many Peacekeepers say that because of this being nice and non-assertive, many unpleasant things are done to them.

Your strength is, at the same time, your biggest pitfall. If you use that too much and not attuned to the other, the other will experience that power negatively and will respond with resistance.

The strengths of the Nine:

- Is neutral

- Does not make impulsive decisions

- Is spiritual

- Blossoms with positive support

- Understands the views of others

- Sets deadlines and a clear structure

- Takes decisions by knowing what he doesn't want

- Avoids anger and conflicts

- Goes with the flow

- Loyalty in relationships

- The ideal mediator

- Does not take unnecessary risks

Response to stress:

Nines try to deal with stress by trivializing their own choices and desires and withdrawing into their inner self. When these skills are insufficient to control their fears, they move to the Six, focusing on relationships and ideas that, they believe, will bring them more certainty and stability. In the event of breakthrough concern and anxiety, Nines focus intensively on their Work and projects.

It is as if, after letting things continue to shake for a while, they suddenly take a jerk into action and try to cover themselves on all sides at the same time in a driven phase of hectic activity. At the same time, they are often extremely reactive towards the demands of others and become highly passive-aggressive and defensive.

Their positive 'philosophy of life' is beginning to show cracks and the doubts and pessimism they have defended are breaking through. Just like Sixes, Nines under stress can bring forward long-hidden complaints about others and their destiny.

Although airing it temporarily reduces their stress, it usually does not really change anything, since they still refuse to be aware of the roots of their unhappiness. They can develop a siege mentality under extreme stress. Paranoid suspicion can quickly escalate into blaming others for their own problems and reacting resolutely. Outbursts of anger and tantrums can come just as surprising for the Nines as for those who witness them.

If Nines have gone through a serious crisis

without adequate support or good coping skills, or if they have been chronically abused in their youth, they can pass the 'shock' point and go behave according to the unhealthy aspects of their type. That may lead them to the frightening insight that the problems and conflicts in their lives will not disappear and perhaps even get worse - mainly because of their inactivity. And their fear may be partly justified. In addition, they could be forced by reality to tackle their problems.

This awareness can be a turning point in the life of the Nine. The moment he sees the truth in these fears, he can take the road to health and liberation. On the other hand, he can become even more stubborn and determined to maintain the comforting illusions that everything is in order.

If the Nine perseveres in this attitude, he can make the fall down to unhealthy levels. If you find yourself or someone you know showing the warning signs (see warning signs) for a longer period of time (longer than a few weeks), then it is highly recommended that you go into therapy or call in other help.

Nines are realized and remain healthy by being aware of their essential nature. In doing so, they overcome their social role, 'Nobody Special', and realize that they are worth their own time and energy. They work on the development of themselves and their potential and move around the world, letting others know what they have to offer.

The greatest obstacle on the way to their self-realization is their tendency towards inertia. Integrating Nines will regularly experience feelings of heaviness or sleepiness as soon as they try to do something good for themselves. But as they integrate more, they also notice that their energy increases and with it their charisma.

Having considered themselves invisible for most of their lives, Integrating Nines are surprised that others not only seem to listen to them but even visit them. Because they recognize their own value, others also value them more. Because they tap into and develop the vitality of their instinctive nature, they energize others.

They can, if necessary, stand up for themselves and realize that self-assertion is not the same as aggression. Moreover, their opposition to reality disappears, making them more flexible and able to respond immediately to their circumstances.

Becoming driven, competitive or image-conscious makes little contribution to building true self-esteem - on the contrary, it will maintain their concern about their own value and keep them dissociated from their true identity.

But when Nines find the energy to take on

their own self-development, love and power of their own hearts become an unbeatable, healing power in their world.

Depending on the situation, the associated degree of stress and the development process that the Nine has gone through, it can express itself at different levels.

Self-Help

Notice when others become the motive for your activity. "Do I agree or disagree with them? Am I joining them or not? "

Provide deadlines, structure, and positive feedback that supports your own goals.

Learn to shift your attention when obsessive thoughts about the pros and cons of a decision prevail.

Focus on your feelings when compulsive thoughts arise. Ask yourself: "What do I want?" Instead of "What do others want?"

Learn to recognize your passive-aggressive signals. Nines exercise control by slowing down and refusing to take action. Recognize this passivity as anger.

See anger as a disguise of something positive. anger can reveal an earlier point of view that you have tucked away.

Nines can make a decision more easily if they are presented with a number of choices. They know better what they do not want than what they do want.

Find out which feelings are numbed by important things such as watching TV, shopping and other ways of not having to take action.